50 Not Out!

50 Not Out!

*A Half Century
of Working in the Field of
Counselling and Psychotherapy*

Windy Dryden, PhD

Onlinevents Publications

First edition published by Onlinevents Publications

Copyright (c) 2025 Windy Dryden and Onlinevents Publications

Windy Dryden
136 Montagu Mansions, London W1U 6LQ

Onlinevents Publications
38 Bates Street, Sheffield, S10 1NQ
www.onlinevents.co.uk
help@onlinevents.co.uk

The right of Windy Dryden and Onlinevents Publications to be
identified as the authors of this work has been asserted in accordance
with sections 77 and 78 of the Copyright Designs and Patents Act
1988.

A catalogue record of this book is
available from the British Library.

First edition 2025

ISBN: 978-1-914938-56-6

Contents

Dedication

This book is dedicated
to my wife, Louise,
whose love and support
have sustained me
throughout my career.

Acknowledgements

Throughout my life and career, many individuals have played a crucial role in my development. Space considerations mean that I can't acknowledge you all. In rough chronological order, thank you:

Mr Lucy, Janet Stockdale, Sheila Chown, Richard Nelson-Jones, John Davis, Marcia Davis, Albert Ellis, Richard Wessler, Ruth Wessler, David Burns, Arnold Lazarus, Peter Trower, Naomi Roth, Jack Gordon, Cassie Cooper, Brian Thorne, Farrell Burnett, David Hill, David Rose, Irene Bloomfield, Stephen Palmer, Michael Neenan, Derek Gale, Steve Weinrach, Joseph Yankura, Colin Whurr, Dom Di Mattia, Kristene Doyle, Ray DiGiuseppe, Walter Matweychuk, Wouter Backx, Joanne Forshaw, Anna Albright, Georgie Aronin, Martin Noble, Swati Khanolkar, Jeff Young (Australia), Christopher Haylock, John Wilson.

Preface

I began my professional career as a counsellor on 1 September 1975. This was when I was appointed Lecturer in Counselling in the Department of Educational Enquiry at the University of Aston in Birmingham. 1 September 2025 will mark fifty years of my work in the field of counselling and psychotherapy, during which time I have held many roles (see Chapter 11). As a writer, I wanted to observe this occasion by publishing a book. The question was: what kind of book? I was clear with myself about what I didn't want to write. I did not want to write an autobiography. I also did not want to write a retrospective account of my development as a therapist and comment on the state of the field. My colleague, Michael Jacobs (2018), has written a book based on his own experiences and views, and he did a much better job than I ever could.

I also did not want to write anything unpleasant about anyone. Albert Ellis said some rather nasty things about me and other people in his autobiography (Ellis, 2009),[1] and I certainly did not want to go down that route. All my mentors had feet of clay, but I have chosen not to elaborate on that point.

I decided, then, to write without a plan and see what happened. Indeed, this is the way my career unfolded. While I was clear that I wanted to be a counsellor, I could never have foreseen how my career would develop, nor could I have predicted that I would write as much as I did. This book, in some ways, mirrors my career development. Things happened to me,

---

[1] See Epilogue, pp. 122–3.

and I responded. They did not happen to me in a logical order, so this book does not have a logical order other than one that reflects the passage of time. What I did want this book to be was personal and short! The obsessive-compulsive part of my personality wanted the book to have fifty chapters and be exactly 50,000 words, but luckily for you, dear reader, I have that part of me firmly in control. The book is as long (or I should say as short) as it needs to be, and I have said all I needed to say.

The book shares memories from my past that are relevant to my personal and professional growth, as well as professional experiences I have found challenging. It also features episodes that have stayed with me and which I believe are worth sharing, alongside my views on key professional concepts and ideas, and a memorable encounter with a client. I hope that by reading this book you gain some insight into what I am like both as a person and as a therapist, and into some of the ideas I cherish about our profession.

Before we begin, let me clarify that in this book I have used the terms 'counsellor', 'therapist', 'counselling' and 'therapy' interchangeably.

Windy Dryden
July 2025
London and Eastbourne

1

'You, Boy! What's Your Name, Boy?' 'It's D-D-D-D-D-David D-D-D-D-D-Denbin'

As a child and teenager, I had a bad stammer. As you might expect, it had quite a negative impact on me. I was reluctant to speak in public, and whenever I did, I would search for words that began with letters that were easy to pronounce without stammering. The letter I had most difficulty saying was 'D', followed by a vowel. Unfortunately, my name (at that time)[2] was David Denbin. I attended an all-boys grammar school, and perhaps unsurprisingly, I was teased for having a stutter. My nickname was 'D-D-D-D'.

One incident that I recall vividly occurred when our class teacher was absent for some reason, and the Deputy Head, a fierce man called Mr Spencer, came into our classroom and told us to be quiet and remain seated. 'Woe betide any boy I catch talking or out of their seats.'

I was a well-behaved boy at school, and I don't remember why I was out of my seat when Mr Spencer returned, but I was.

'You, boy! What's your name, boy?' he bellowed.

'It's D-D-D-D-D-David D-D-D-D-D-Denbin,' I replied.

I do remember Mr Spencer's tone softening after I finally managed to tell him my name.

---

[2] I changed my name later, as I will explain.

A similar situation occurred when a teacher's kindness backfired. This concerned the Headmaster, Mr Cowan, who took us for elocution lessons. At the end of every lesson, two boys had to speak out loud a short piece with an English accent, a Welsh accent and a Scottish accent. There were thirty boys in our class, and nobody knew who would be chosen to recite the piece that started, 'When Peter got to the gate....'

At every lesson with Mr Cowan, I was anxious in case it was my turn. As it turned out, Mr Cowan did not call on me to read aloud to the class. My hunch was that he was trying to spare me from the discomfort and embarrassment of stammering in front of everyone in the class. If that was the case, he was being kind. However, I was anxious every week for fifteen weeks in case this was the week I would be picked. If only he had said to me, 'Denbin, I know you have a stammer and you will find reading aloud to the class difficult. We can either agree that you don't have to do it or we can agree on a date when you will do it. What would you prefer?' But this was the early 1960s, and grammar school headmasters did not believe in consulting their pupils on such matters. So, Mr Cowan's kindness in sparing me discomfort and embarrassment made me feel needlessly anxious for fifteen weeks.

So, what has all this got to do with therapy?

First, having a stammer made me aware of my internal world. I learned what it felt like to be anxious and what that anxiety was about: stammering and being judged for it. In addition to learning about anxiety, I also learned about hurt. On several occasions, a boy who would be friendly with me when we were alone together would later join in with other boys teasing me for my stammer. Such changes in stance towards me were hurtful.

Second, what I am calling here the 'kindness of teachers' taught me to look beneath the fierce and distant stances of these two teachers and see kindness, a wish to soothe me in the first place and spare me pain in the second place. Of course, these were only glimpses, but they were sufficient to leave a lasting impression.

In therapy, we often seek the reasons behind our clients' issues, and yes, we can say that these experiences may have been formative in leading me to want to help people. However, I could have had those experiences without wanting to become a counsellor. I just don't know. What I do know is that experiences like these have taught me to be curious about people's past experiences as contributing factors to their current concerns, but I don't see them as the cause of these issues. Hence my interest in therapies that help people look forward, rather than backwards, unless they want to discuss their past.

2

Goon, But Not Forgotten

When I was a boy, help for people who stammered was quite basic. I visited an NHS speech therapist who taught me the 'easy bounce' method of speaking. This technique, when working with individuals who stammer, aims to lessen tension and encourage smoother speech by making the initial contact of speech sounds lighter and more relaxed. It involves deliberately making the repetitions or prolongations of sounds gentler and less forceful, enabling the speaker to navigate moments of stuttering with greater ease and less struggle.

This method can be utilised as a stuttering modification technique to enhance fluency and minimise the impact of stuttering on communication. For example, my speech therapist suggested that when telling people my name, rather than saying, 'My name is David Denbin' and stammering when coming to my name, I should say, 'M-m-m-m-my n-n-n-n-name i-i-i-i-is D-D-D-D-David D-D-D-D-Denbin.

Now, picture a fifteen-year-old boy who is already being teased at school for stammering. Will I use the 'easy bounce' method when talking? I don't think so.

This taught me an important lesson as a therapist years later. Always check with a client that they can see themself using a technique in their own life rather than assume that they will once they have been taught the method. I remember one of my mentors (Albert Ellis) humorously telling me that he had invented the most effective smoking cessation method ever. Every time you light a cigarette, put the lit end into your mouth. The trouble was, Ellis said, nobody would ever use it.

Once I decided that I would not use the 'easy bounce' method, I gave up on NHS speech therapy, and my parents paid for me to have private speech therapy with a woman living in Stamford Hill called Mrs Cosman. She taught me to speak 'on the breath', as she called it, which had greater face validity for me than the 'easy bounce' method, and I used it in real life to the best of my ability. This improved my fluency a little, but I was still anxious about speaking in public.

Being anxious, I would use a variety of methods designed to reduce my anxiety. Thus, I would avoid speaking in public whenever possible. When I had to speak, I would avoid using words that began with a hard consonant followed by a vowel, hence the problem with my name (David Denbin), or I would omit the consonant altogether (e.g., 'My name is Avid Enbin, but they both begin with a D'). This latter strategy brought me more quizzical attention than if I stammered! I continued in this vein for several years.

Then, in my late teens, I heard a radio interview with one of the Goons, Michael Bentine, who went on to develop and host a television programme called *Michael Bentine's Potty Time*. During that hour-long interview, Bentine spent a couple of minutes talking about his stammer and how he overcame it. He said that a Wigmore Street speech therapist named Harry Burgess helped him through the psychological as well as physical challenges to speaking more clearly with confidence, and, eventually, it worked.

In particular, he said that what helped him was the attitude that he developed towards stammering, which was, 'If I stammer, I stammer – too bad.' This comment particularly resonated with me, and it made perfect sense. I could see how my attitude impacted how I approached speaking in public. This psychological component was absent from all the help I received from the NHS and Mrs Cosman.

Armed with my new attitude, I decided to use every opportunity to speak in public and refrain from using my word substitution technique. Initially, and perhaps unsurprisingly, I became more anxious and stammered more frequently, but by persisting in my approach, I gradually became less anxious and stammered less. By implementing what I learned from a two-minute segment of an hour-long radio interview with Michael Bentine, I had helped myself enormously. I recount this story in my training courses on single-session therapy as a personal example of the potential therapeutic power of a brief encounter with another person.

Another thing that helped me during this period was learning to 'dis-identify' from my stammer. Instead of viewing myself as 'a stammerer', which links my identity to my stammer, I began to see myself as someone who is fluent most of the time and only stammers occasionally. This approach does not tie my identity to stammering and is also more factually accurate.

Years later, when I became a practitioner of Rational Emotive Behaviour Therapy, I could see that the attitude that I learned from Michael Bentine, 'If I stammer, I stammer – too bad', was an example of what REBT calls 'a non-awfulising attitude' and that the dis-identifying method described above was consistent with REBT's view that the self is highly complex and defies a single global rating.

As I note in Chapter 7, it is essential that therapists personally apply and integrate into their own lives what they teach, both explicitly and implicitly, to their clients.

3

'There Are Only Two Kinds of Lawyers: Rich Ones and Millionaires'

At school, I showed a flair for languages. The way languages were taught in the 1960s placed a strong emphasis on translating texts rather than on conversation. Given that I had a stammer, this emphasis suited me quite well, and I ended up studying French, Russian and Latin at A-level. At this time, the school encouraged us to start thinking about our future vocational goals. It occurred to me that while I was good at languages, this talent was not enough to become a translator and certainly not to be an interpreter, even if I did not have a stammer.

After discussing it with the careers master at school, I decided that I wanted to become a psychologist, and to achieve that, I needed to study Psychology at university. I went home and discussed it with my parents. My mother was supportive, but my father was less so.

Let me put my father's response into context. He grew up in the East End of London and was the elder of two brothers of immigrant Jewish parents who could not speak English. My father was expected to leave school early to contribute to the family finances, which he did. He was an intelligent man and a talented artist who had to sacrifice his career prospects for the sake of his family.

My father became a presser in a firm that made clothes for women. He also trained as a gents hairdresser and worked on Saturdays in a barber shop. Later, when I was fourteen, he trained as a London taxi driver. He was an incredibly hard-working man and wanted something very different for me, his only child.

So, when I told him I wanted to become a psychologist, he seemed disappointed.

'I was hoping that you would want to become a lawyer,' he said.

'Why?' I replied.

'Because there are only two kinds of lawyers: rich ones and millionaires.'

When I said I had no interest in law, he looked puzzled.

'But if you become a lawyer, you will be financially secure for life,' he said.

For my father, having a profession with good financial prospects was the primary priority for his son, while being interested in what one does was secondary. For me, being interested in your career was the primary focus, with good financial prospects coming second.

This book celebrates fifty years of my work in counselling and psychotherapy. I am fairly sure that I would not have reached this milestone without a genuine passion, let alone interest, in this field. Although I have earned a good living over the years, I have not fulfilled my father's aspirations in this regard. Nonetheless, I love my work and have no immediate plans to retire.

4

Shotgun

I mentioned in Chapter 1 that some therapists like to explore a client's past to understand the reasons for their current behaviour. I have never truly resonated with this approach. While it is always possible to find such 'explanations', they may not carry much real weight. Perhaps the key is what the client believes to be true, rather than whether it is actually true. As George Kelly (1955), the founder of personal construct psychology, explained, a person's own meaning and definition form the basis of who they are and shape their perspective of the world based on their individual constructs. However, sometimes we don't know, and it's important to accept the wondrous nature of not knowing. Let me provide a personal example to illustrate this latter point.

In April 1965, I was sitting in my parents' kitchen in Hackney, East London, listening to the radio. Suddenly, I heard the crack of a rifle, the roll of drums, and the sound of a raunchy saxophone that captured my full attention. I was listening to 'Shotgun' by Jr. Walker and the All Stars. Sixty years later, I still get goosebumps when I hear that track. Now here's the question: why did a young, white, fifteen-year-old Jewish boy from the East End of London resonate so completely with a track written and performed by a black, thirty-four-year-old man from Battle Creek, Michigan?

I don't know the answer, and for me, trying to find one takes some of the wonder away. I am happy to accept that in my life, the answer to such questions as, why do I like Gregorian Monk Chants, the films of the Marx Brothers, the ghost stories of M.R.

James and many other things is: 'I don't know, and it is of little importance to me to find out.' I accept the mysterious and enigmatic nature of such matters and just enjoy them.

In therapy, clients sometimes ask why they are the way they are. My response is to ask them whether answering this question will help them deal with the issue that is troubling them at the moment. If it will, then I am happy to assist them in finding an answer that will help them do so, rather than one that merely reflects 'reality'. If not, then we can focus on helping them address the factors that contribute to the problem, so I can assist them in making it a non-issue.   Sometimes, I ask clients if they want to hear my response to their question about why they are the way they are. If they do, here is my answer:

'You have been exposed to many different potential influences on your development, and you also bring internal processes, such as your temperament, to these influences. It is impossible to answer your question with any degree of validity, so I invite you to accept the wondrous nature of the unknown and the unknowable and the wondrous complexity of yourself as a unique person.'

Then I play them 'Shotgun' by Jr. Walker and the All Stars and tell them my story, just as I have told it to you.

5

Is Windy Dryden My Real Name?

One of the downsides of having an unusual first name is that people either keep commenting on it (e.g., 'Windy, that's an unusual name') or asking if it is my real name. Some use it to show what they consider to be their humour ('Were you born on a windy day'? or 'Did your parents live next to the Heinz baked beans factory'?[3] Depending on how I am feeling at the time, I may choose to explain the name or make a flippant comment (e.g. 'My name is Lord Windlesham III, but I don't like to brag').

Now, let me put the record straight.

As I have explained, I used to have a bad stammer and had particular difficulty saying the name that appears on my birth certificate: David Denbin. In the mid-1960s, inspired by 'Shotgun' by Jr. Walker and the All Stars, I began to learn how to play the saxophone. Unfortunately, I was not very good and was given the nickname 'Windy'.

I dropped out of the University of Nottingham after three weeks and spent six months on a kibbutz in Israel. At that time, David was a common name, especially for young Jewish men, and as there were several 'Davids' on that kibbutz, most of us were encouraged to come up with an alternative name. I chose 'Windy'. On my return to England, I decided to change my name legally. And given that I still struggled to say my first name and surname without stammering, I decided to change both my

---

[3] For my younger readers, eating baked beans is supposed to lead to flatulence. Windy, flatulence, get it? As Frankie Howerd used to say, 'Please yourself.'

names. During the six months I spent in Israel, I had grown accustomed to being called Windy and quite liked it. But what to choose for a surname?

At that time, the first part of telephone numbers (the telephone exchange) was a name rather than a number. At that time, I lived with my parents in Kenton, Middlesex, and our telephone exchange was called 'Dryden', so I decided to select 'Dryden'[4] as my new surname. So, I became Windy Dryden. Where we lived, telephone exchanges were named after literary figures, and latterly, I have joked that if I had lived a few streets to the left, my name would have been Windy Wordsworth and to the right, Windy Shakespeare.

So, yes, Windy Dryden is my real, legal name, and no, it was not the name I was given at birth.

And no, I am not Lord Windlesham III!

---

[4] While 'Dryden' begins with the letter 'D' the 'r' that follows softens it and made it easy for me to say it without stammering.

6

Dipping In and Out with People and Autonomy: Matters of Temperament

One implication of what I mentioned in Chapter 4 is that it is crucial to accept the existence of what you do not understand instead of fighting against it internally and externally. If you can change it and wish to, do so; if not, move on.

One of the things about myself that I have come to recognise and accept is that I am fundamentally a loner. I enjoy being on my own. Does that mean I am anti-social or non-social? Not at all. Instead, I enjoy the company of others, but in small doses – small in time and small in number. In addition, I am an autonomously organised individual.

I enjoy making my own decisions and forging my own path without having to account to others. By dint of this fact, I should have been self-employed for all my working life, but I also sought the security of a regular salary and a good pension. Although my father was wrong to suggest that I sacrifice my interests for great wealth, I think he would have been pleased that I was financially secure.

While I have always done a variety of professional tasks (see Chapter 11), I have only had two full-time jobs – at the University of Aston in Birmingham from 1975 to 1983 and at Goldsmiths University of London from 1985 to 2014. Fortunately, academic life provided me with the context that allowed me to be autonomous and yet gave me enough social contact to satisfy me.

I managed to limit my attendance at staff meetings, particularly in the latter years and did not serve on many academic committees. I once took a values test, which showed that my number one value was 'autonomy' and my least favourite value was 'working in teams'. While there are value aspects to both characteristics, I regard them more as matters of temperament. Being able to accept myself for my temperament has been satisfying, but years earlier in my life I thought that being insufficiently social meant that there was something wrong with me.

I explored this in personal therapy, and it would have been good if my therapist had reassured me that this was an issue of temperament, but he didn't and embarked on a search for a psychodynamic explanation of my lack of sociability. This reinforced the idea that there was something wrong with me.

It was only later, and without the help of a therapist, that I accepted that I am a loner. While I enjoy being in the company of others, I prefer one-to-one contact, and when I spend time with a group, it needs to be small. Additionally, I recognise that I like to dip in and out of interpersonal contact with small groups. It should not be lost on you, dear reader, that a fifty-minute therapeutic hour with breaks between sessions suits me very well!

My acceptance of myself for these temperamental factors made me aware of the role of temperament in people's development, and I encourage my clients to reflect on the part that such factors play in their lives.

7

Finding My Therapeutic Home

Having decided I wanted to study Psychology at university, I applied through the usual process and received an offer to study a BA in Psychology and Philosophy at the University of Nottingham, which I accepted. However, when I arrived in September 1968, I quickly realised that Philosophy was not for me, and the university permitted me to switch to a BA in Psychology. Nevertheless, I was terribly homesick and decided to leave after three weeks.

Instead, I spent six months at Kibbutz Matsuva, a kibbutz located north of Nahariya in Israel, near the Lebanese border. Here, I joined a group of Jewish eighteen-year-olds on Ulpan.[5] In effect, we were all having a gap year between school and university. This experience helped me to grow up, and on my return to England, I was better prepared to begin my university studies. In September 1969, I attended the London School of Economics to study for a BSc in Social Psychology, a new course that had begun that year.

Three years later, I emerged with an upper second and decided to do a PhD, which I did at Bedford College, which was part of the University of London, and located in Regents Park.[6] I was awarded the higher degree after two years of intense study. During the five years I spent studying in London, I worked as a

---

[5] On Ulpan, half the day we learned Hebrew and the other half we worked, usually picking oranges, clearing up chicken shit or in the kitchens.
[6] This is now Regents College.

Samaritan and a Nightline counsellor and discovered that I enjoyed helping people. Therefore, when considering my career options after completing my PhD, I decided to apply for and was accepted into the one-year Diploma in Counselling in Educational Settings at the University of Aston in Birmingham.

This course focused on client-centred therapy,[7] though we also studied other key therapeutic approaches of that time. I connected with the theory of client-centred therapy, but I struggled with its practical application, which I found too restrictive and was not closely aligned with my personality. Afterwards, I received training in psychodynamic therapy at the Uffculme Clinic in Birmingham, but I neither resonated with its theory nor its practice.

New York and Warwick

At that point, I felt unclear about my direction as a therapist. I knew I did not want to practise client-centred or psychodynamic therapy, but I was unsure of what approach I did want to practise. When reviewing the methods we studied on the Aston course, I felt most closely aligned with what was then called Rational-Emotive Therapy[8] and decided to travel to New York in the summer of 1978 to undertake intensive training in this method at the Institute for Rational-Emotive Therapy.[9] In September 1978, I started a two-year MSc in Psychotherapy at the University of Warwick. The training I received in REBT provided the depth I was seeking, while the education at Warwick offered the breadth

---

[7] Later, in 1980, this became known as person-centred therapy.
[8] Later, in 1993, this became known as Rational Emotive Behaviour Therapy.
[9] Later, this became known as the Albert Ellis Institute.

I needed. By the end of these two programmes, the therapist I was in 1980 was very different from the one in 1978.

The way I thought about it then and how I still think about it is that I found my therapeutic home. I resonated with both the theory and practice of REBT. Remember from Chapter 2 how I addressed my anxiety about stammering. In retrospect, what I did then was very closely aligned with REBT. I took the horror, but not the badness, out of stammering and applied this attitude while acting in ways that were consistent with it.

Eventually, I lost my anxiety about speaking in public. I later wrote a chapter for an excellent book edited by Ernesto Spinelli and Sue Marshall on what they called 'embodied theory' in which I explored how the theory and practice of REBT informed the way I lived my life in relevant areas. As it turned out, REBT showed up in many of these (Dryden, 2001a).

The education I received at Warwick introduced me to the concepts of eclecticism, integration and working alliance theory, which have informed my practice ever since. So, while I can say that my major therapeutic allegiance is to REBT, my practice of it is very broad.

Single-Session Therapy (SST)

In 2014, I retired from my role at Goldsmiths, University of London, and started contemplating my next challenge. In doing so, I revisited the activities I found most enjoyable throughout my varied professional career (see Chapter 11). This was performing live demonstrations before an audience (Dryden, 2021a). Consequently, I developed an interest in single-session therapy (Talmon, 1990), which has now become my second therapeutic home (see Chapter 21).

Conclusion

My view is that therapists need to practise in ways with which
they resonate. This is a slightly different take on the concept of
therapeutic congruence. I am referring to the congruence
between the therapist and the way they practise. However, it is
vital that this 'therapeutic home', as I am calling it here, is broad
enough to reflect the fact that clients are very different from one
another and come to counselling for different things. I have two
therapeutic homes – REBT (Dryden, 2021b) and SST. I also have
a very big garden which currently comprises pluralism[10] (Cooper
& McLeod, 2011) and working alliance theory[11] (Bordin, 1979).

---

[10] See Chapter 10.
[11] See Chapter 8.

8

The Importance of the Working Alliance

One of the concepts that we learned about on the Warwick course that has stayed with me throughout my career as a therapist, trainer and supervisor and that has had a profound effect on that career is Ed Bordin's (1979) reformulation of the psychoanalytic concept of the working alliance.[12] Indeed, we were lucky to have Bordin as a guest lecturer during the course when he was visiting the UK.

I was trained in client-centred therapy at Aston in 1974–75, as I mentioned in the previous chapter, and, of course, read Carl Rogers' work, including his seminal article, which set out his views on the centrality of the therapeutic relationship in counselling and psychotherapy (Rogers, 1957). In brief, Rogers stressed that when a client experiences their therapist as regarding them positively and unconditionally, as empathic with respect to their frame of reference, and as genuine in their encounters with them, then positive therapeutic change will inevitably occur.

Most of the training at Aston focused on helping us, as budding counsellors, to demonstrate these conditions. This, despite Rogers' (1957) caution that the critical factor was not the

---

[12] The 'working alliance' is sometimes referred to as the 'therapeutic alliance' and occasionally in my own writings I have used this latter term, However, in this book, and to honour Bordin's work, I will use the term 'working alliance'. It also indicates that there is work to be done.

therapist's *demonstration* of these conditions, but the client's *experience* of them. Nevertheless, when I began the Warwick course, I was primed to see the importance of the therapeutic relationship.

I found Bordin's ideas on the working alliance richer and more comprehensive than Rogers' writings on the therapist–client relationship. Basically, Bordin argued that three domains comprise the working alliance: Bonds, Goals and Tasks.

Bonds

Therapeutic bonds point to the interconnectedness between client and therapist. The way I think about bonds is that they are made up of two crucial components: the core conditions and collaboration.

Core Conditions

The core conditions reflect Rogers' (1957) view of what is therapeutic about the relationship between client and therapist, as discussed above. My view is that these are important ingredients but are neither necessary nor sufficient for therapeutic change to occur, a view echoed by Ellis (1959) in his rebuttal of Rogers' (1957) paper. Furthermore, I believe that for some clients, certain conditions are more critical than for others and, for a particular client, one or more of these conditions may be more important at certain times than at others.

Collaboration

Collaboration between the therapist and client focuses on how effectively they work together in therapy. It is popularly thought that collaboration is shown by the rough equality of the amount that the client and therapist speak in a session and indeed this is one important marker of collaboration. However, for example, it may be that when a therapist is quite active and the client relatively passive, the client is learning more than they would if they were more active. Here, if the therapist urges them to be more active, they may collaborate and learn less. This points to the importance of the therapeutic style that both client and therapist adopt in sessions. Does this relational style between them promote or impede client learning? This, for me, is the key question.

Goals

Goals are the core purpose of therapy. Clients come to therapy for a reason, even if they are not entirely clear what this reason is. Many years ago, Alvin Mahrer (1967) compiled a significant book on therapy goals. He invited renowned therapists of the day to discuss their perspectives on therapy goals. Analysing their responses, Mahrer suggested that therapists generally have two main aims: to alleviate suffering and to foster growth.

In my view, while it is essential for therapists to acknowledge that they have goals in doing the work, it is equally important for them to discover what their clients' goals are. There has been much written on clients' goals in therapy (e.g., Cooper & Law, 2018) and I will not review this material here. What I will say is that the more the client can be helped to express their goals with clarity and specificity and to indicate the presence of healthy responses as goals rather than the absence of unhealthy responses, the better. Given my interest in single-session therapy, I am also keen to help clients to set goals for the session as well goals for the end of therapy.

From an alliance perspective what is therapeutic is that the client and therapist agree on the former's goals.

Tasks

Tasks represent activities undertaken by the therapist and client inside therapy sessions and by the client outside therapy sessions that have a bearing on the therapeutic outcome for that client.[13] Several questions become salient when looking at the tasks domain of the working alliance. These include:

1. Does the client understand their tasks in therapy (both inside and outside sessions); do they agree to carry them out and can they do so?
2. Does the client understand the therapist's tasks in therapy and agree with them?
3. Is the therapist skilled in executing their tasks?
4. Are the tasks that the client carries out potent enough to promote desired changes?
5. Are the therapist and client working in a way that demonstrates that their tasks are 'in sync'?

---

[13] In this section, I won't discuss tasks undertaken by the therapist outside therapy sessions (such as personal therapy, supervision, and continuous professional development activities) since they are harder to relate to the outcome of therapy for a specific client.

Meta-therapy Communication as a Key Task in Therapy

I believe that an essential role for both the therapist and client is their openness and capacity to talk about their collaborative work. This process is often known as 'meta-therapy communication'. In this context, one party indicates that there's a concern regarding therapy that needs to be raised with the other. Once this channel of communication is set up successfully, it becomes the space where significant issues related to the client's therapy can be dealt with. For instance, it provides a platform to discuss and resolve therapeutic ruptures.

Views

Although Bordin's work has had a profound influence on the way I think about and practise counselling, I found it lacking in one crucial respect. It did not deal with the understandings that the therapist and client have about the practical and therapeutic issues relating to their work. Thus I published a book entitled *Counselling in a Nutshell*, in which I suggested an additional domain that I called 'Views' to take these understandings into account (Dryden, 2006, 2011). On the basis that shared understandings between client and therapist are therapeutic, the following is a list of views that need to be mutually understood and agreed on.

Views on Practical Issues

- The therapist's fee, and when and how it is to be paid
- Where therapy is to take place and whether the therapist has waiting facilities

- If therapy is to take place online, what is the etiquette that the client needs to follow (e.g. dress, location, privacy)?
- The therapist's cancellation policy
- The therapist's confidentiality policy
- How the therapeutic contract is to be made
- The length of therapy sessions

Views on Therapeutic Issues

- The length of therapy
- Views of the client's problem(s) and relevant explanatory factors
- Views of how the client's problem(s) are to be addressed
- Views of what the client is expected to do between sessions
- Views related to the ending of therapy

For readers interested to learn about research into the working alliance, I recommend Flückiger, Del Re, Wampold and Horvath (2018).

9

54 Job Rejections and Zero Self-Rejections[14]

In this chapter, I return to a time in my life (1983–85) when I was struggling. In doing so, I will outline my experiences after I took voluntary redundancy from my university position as Lecturer in Counselling at the University of Aston in Birmingham in July 1983 and was appointed in August 1985 Senior Lecturer in Psychology at what is now Goldsmiths University of London.

In 1981, Aston University faced approximately a 31% reduction in its funding. These cuts significantly affected the Department of Educational Enquiry, where I was a lecturer. This department hosted the well-established one-year Postgraduate Diploma in Counselling in Educational Settings course, on which I served as Course Tutor from 1977 onward.

Before Aston University received the 'infamous' letter announcing the cuts from the University Grants Committee, the Department of Educational Enquiry was a vibrant unit with sixteen staff members, producing high quality research. The department offered two postgraduate programmes and a successful undergraduate course in human communication, which was quite new at the time. Due to internal conflicts triggered by the UGC letter, the department was directed to cut its staff from sixteen to six. It achieved this only after several long-standing staff members chose early retirement or accepted

---

14 This is an updated version of a piece published in Dryden (1993).

voluntary redundancy schemes that the university rapidly introduced.

After the department reached its six-staff target, it underwent an independent external review. The verdict was that it was 'too small' to support meaningful educational activities. Subsequently, staff members were interviewed by the Vice-Chancellor and offered new positions. I was given the chance to join the Manpower Management and Legal Studies Group at the Management Centre, a move that caused confusion for myself and others in that group.

At that time, the responsibility for managing the counselling course was transferred to the centre, which immediately resulted in the termination of secretarial support. I faced the challenge of running the course alone, without secretarial help or genuine support from the centre, despite their promises. Additionally, I had to personally fund secretarial assistance. It seemed that my long-term prospects at the university were quite uncertain, especially since few people within the Management Centre showed any interest in counselling, and there were indications that the counselling course would soon be altered to better align with that part of the university's ethos.

A new redundancy scheme was introduced, offering staff a lump sum of £26,000. I chose to accept voluntary redundancy, especially since I was also offered the incentive to return part-time the next year to teach on the counselling course. I left my full-time role at the university in July 1983, making sure that the Management Centre's office coordinated the necessary tutorial support for the Diploma students in the upcoming year.

Looking back, I think that returning to Aston University part-time in October 1983 was a mistake. I found it more challenging than expected to handle the stress of becoming an external part-time lecturer, having previously been deeply involved in the Course as Course Tutor. I was caught in a dilemma: on one side, I wanted to intervene because I felt the students were being somewhat neglected by the Management Centre; on the other side, I knew that such intervention was not part of my paid duties. Additionally, with a new Course Tutor in place, it seemed best to stay out of internal university matters. I couldn't resolve this dilemma and fluctuated between these two positions throughout that academic year.

As part of my 'leaving package', I participated in a career-counselling programme arranged by a private consultancy contracted by Aston University. The programme aimed to assist those accepting voluntary redundancy in exploring future career options. I chose to take part, because it was free, and in the hope it would help me restart my career.

At the time, I believed I wouldn't be unemployed for long, trusting that my academic background, training and clinical experience would make it easy to find another full-time position. I expected that by June 1984, when my part-time contract with Aston University ended, I would have secured new employment-though not necessarily within academia.

The career counselling helped clarify what I didn't want to do but also had its disadvantages. It prompted me to create a polished, industry-specific CV, which, as I later realised, was less effective with academic institutions and training or counselling agencies. Eventually, I realised that my initial hope of a quick return to full employment was too optimistic, and I began to accept that I might need to go on unemployment benefits, which I did in June 1984.

I was unemployed from June 1984 until November 1984, which made me eligible for the Government's Enterprise

Allowance Scheme. This scheme provided a financial incentive for people to start their own self-employment venture that was more advantageous than remaining on unemployment benefits. In November 1984, I officially established my own Consultation and Training business in Counselling Psychology. Still, I viewed this as a temporary step until I secured another full-time role. That opportunity came in March 1985 when I was appointed as a Senior Lecturer in Psychology at what is now Goldsmiths University of London, starting the position in August 1985.

From the time I left Aston University in July 1983 until I was appointed to my position at Goldsmiths in March 1985, I submitted 55 job applications. An analysis of these applications and the interviews I attended is presented in Table 1.

Table 1 Analysis of job applications and interviews:
July 1983-March 1985

Application Type	Number of Applications	Number of Interviews
Lectureships - Counselling - Psychology	13	6
Practitioner posts	15	6
Administrative positions – in the helping professions	10	3
Training posts	3	0
Research posts	1	1
Clinical psychology training courses - Applying as a student to be retrained	13	5
Total	55	21

Generally, my experiences of applying and interviewing for counselling and related roles were that it was quite rare to receive reliable feedback on why I failed to be shortlisted or failed to be offered the job after interview. I stopped asking for such feedback after a while because few organisations showed genuine sensitivity or care during interviews. A notable exception was the Student Counselling Service at the University of Lancaster, which behaved professionally, empathetically and in a dignified manner in line with counselling standards.

I also encountered unpleasant experiences; for example, at a College of Further Education, candidates weren't offered coffee during a day-long interview but were simply pointed to a coffee machine that only accepted ten-pence coins. My most discouraging moment was during a counselling lecturer interview at an Institute of Higher Education, where none of the three candidates, including me, were hired. We were told that our teaching experience was insufficient for the Lecturer II level, although it was hinted that if any of us would accept a Lecturer I position, we might be offered the job. Given my background as a lecturer and trainer, I found this insulting.

During the two years between leaving my position at Aston and starting at Goldsmiths, I believe I handled the situation quite well. It's worth noting that I faced no financial difficulties during this time because I had invested my £26,000 lump sum from Aston University and was living off the interest. Additionally, my wife was employed full-time as a teacher in Birmingham throughout this period.

How I Dealt with Unemployment and the Difficulty of Finding a Job

On a personal level, I applied principles from Rational Emotive Behaviour Therapy to my situation. I didn't experience depression during this period and accepted my unemployed status.

When I got rejected for a position, I refused to devalue myself. As I am now fond of saying, 'I had 54 job rejections and zero self-rejections!' I regularly reviewed my strengths, particularly after failing to secure any of the 21 positions I interviewed for. Later, I received useful feedback that my confidence in interviews sometimes came across as arrogance. Interestingly, I was offered a position at an interview where I felt most anxious.

I occasionally felt destructive anger, especially regarding how I was treated at the Institute of Higher Education mentioned earlier. However, I realised that although I believed I deserved better treatment, staff didn't have to treat me well during interviews, even if I preferred it. Despite occasional doubts about finding another job, I mostly believed I would eventually find something to which I could commit, viewing self-employment as a temporary option.

Overall, I coped fairly well and didn't feel the need for personal counselling. I relied on my own coping skills and appreciated support from important people, especially my wife Louise, who was very supportive and respected how I paced myself over these two years. I also appreciated the fact that my family and friends didn't constantly ask about my job applications but trusted me to share what I chose. Interestingly, some in the counselling field found it difficult not to try to counsel me, which I didn't need at the time! Looking back, I believe that writing was one of my most therapeutic activities during this period. It was both my most productive and creative phase, partly because I had the time for it. Writing kept me engaged in something creative and made me feel I was still contributing professionally, which I never felt I had left (see Chapter 30).

In summary, the period from accepting voluntary redundancy to starting at Goldsmiths University of London can be summed up as: 'It was a valuable experience, I'm glad I had it, but I wouldn't want to repeat it!'

10

Theoretically Consistent Eclecticism and Pluralism

In Chapter 5, I explained that my Master's in Psychotherapy at the University of Warwick introduced me to the ideas of eclecticism and psychotherapy integration. I also stated there that my first therapeutic approach was Rational Emotive Behaviour Therapy. Dissatisfied with REBT therapists' limited intervention options, I sought to include techniques from other therapies, ensuring they aligned with REBT principles. I termed this approach 'theoretically consistent eclecticism' (Dryden, 1987).

When individuals identify as integrative therapists, they typically mean they blend multiple approaches into a cohesive whole. Given that this process is not often clear, I often inquire about what they aim to integrate and what they omit. I haven't felt connected to this type of psychotherapy integration since I am not particularly interested in developing an approach to therapy that is cohesively whole. Instead, I find myself aligning more with the concept of pluralism (Cooper & McLeod, 2011; Cooper & Dryden, 2016) particularly as a way of looking at matters therapeutic.

What Is Pluralism?

Pluralism can be defined as the philosophical belief that 'any substantial question admits of a variety of plausible but mutually conflicting responses' (Rescher, 1993: 79). It shows a commitment to valuing diversity and suspicion of single, all embracing 'truths'. Cooper (2019) distinguished between holding a pluralistic perspective on therapy and pluralistic practice.

I would say that I do hold a pluralistic perspective on therapy which, as Cooper says, is about adopting a general attitude of acceptance and valuing towards the entire array of therapeutic approaches without committing to practising all of them. I would say, though, that my practice of REBT is still best described as theoretically consistent eclecticism as discussed above rather than pluralistic practice since as Cooper says there is still an emphasis in this form of practice in developing a coherent whole, which as I have said above, I am not interested in.

The Principles of Pluralism

So, what are the principles that comprise the pluralistic perspective as defined above?

In my view, the following are key principles of pluralism:

- There is no one absolute right way of understanding clients' problems and solutions – different viewpoints are useful for different clients.
- There is no one absolute right way of practising therapy – different clients need different things and therefore need to have a broad practice repertoire.
- Disputes and disagreements in the field of psychotherapy, in part, can be resolved by taking a 'both-and' perspective, rather than an 'either/or' one.

- It is important that therapists respect each other's work and recognise the value that that work can have.
- Therapists should ideally acknowledge and celebrate clients' diversity and uniqueness.
- Clients should ideally be involved fully throughout the therapy process.
- Clients should ideally be understood in terms of their strengths and resources as well as their areas of struggle.
- Therapists should ideally have an openness to multiple sources of knowledge on how to practise therapy: including research, personal experience, and theory.
- It is important that therapists take a critical perspective on their own theory and practice: being willing to look at their own investment in a particular position and having the ability to stand back from it.

Examples of Pluralistic Practice in Single-Session Therapy

As I will discuss more extensively in Chapter 21, my second therapeutic home is single-session therapy. In my view, the publication of Moshe Talmon's (1990) book was a key moment in the development of SST worldwide. Talmon (2018: 153) provided the following examples of what I deem to show that in in SST we take a pluralistic perspective and why I have written that pluralism is a good framework to underpin SST (Dryden, 2024a). Talmon calls the following 'dynamic poles' in SST. He says that he may take what appear to be opposite positions, but they should be regarded as both-and rather than either/or:

- Validating a patient's story via empathic listening and challenging the problematic elements in the same storyline.
- Increasing a sense of hope or a realistic sense of optimism and helping a person to accept certain parts of the harsh reality.
- Offering neutral (and at times passive, silent) listening in one part of a session, and in another part, presenting active, focused questions.
- Being non-directive at one point of the session, and at other times giving prescriptive-like directions.

While I have not been an active part of the movement in pluralism in therapy,[15] I am a supporter of the movement's endeavours, and I am happy to say that I am guided by the pluralistic principles listed above.

---

[15] Although I did co-edit a book on the subject with Mick Cooper (Cooper & Dryden, 2016).

11

Variety Is the Spice of My Working Life

By the time this book has been published, I would have celebrated fifty years working in the field of counselling and psychotherapy. While this is not a unique achievement – my erstwhile colleague, Michael Jacobs (2018) achieved this milestone seven years ago – there are not many people who have worked in this field for fifty years, and in my case continue to do so. So, what is the secret of my longevity? As I discussed in Chapter 3, I ignored my father's suggestion that I become a lawyer to secure my future financial security on the grounds that I was not interested in the law. I knew then that I would have made a terrible decision if I had followed my father's advice. My view then, as it is now, was that it is vital that I am interested in the work that I do and that this work is aligned with my core values. For me helping people lead as lives as mentally healthy as possible is one of my core values.

However, I am sure that if I had only worked as a therapist or counsellor and did nothing else that I would have lasted nowhere near fifty years in the field. I do not do well only doing one thing. For me, what is important is the variety of different tasks that I have undertaken in the field. Variety has been the spice of my working life.

Here are the ten roles that I have occupied in the field: (i) individual therapist, (ii) couples therapist, (iii) group therapist, (iv) trainer, (v) supervisor, (vi) writer of books, book chapters and journal articles on my own and in collaboration with others, (vii) editor of books, book series and journals,[16] (viii) course director, (ix) researcher and (x) director of a group-based CBT programme. Of course, I have not held all these roles at the same time, but I have never only occupied one such role. In my view, in particular, my work as a trainer and supervisor of therapists has enhanced my work as a practitioner and vice versa.

Although I have never worked full-time as a therapist, as noted above, it is my firm view that if people stop seeing clients, they should also stop supervising and training therapists and should also stop writing about the subject if they been doing so. I have seen too many people continue to supervise and train therapists once they have stopped seeing clients and I will publicly declare here that I will not do so. Once I stop practising, I will retire from all the other roles that I have occupied and enumerated above (see the Epilogue).

Nevertheless, I feel that retirement is still a long way off, although of course, the future is unpredictable. For now, I will keep practising, training, supervising and writing, and I will enjoy each of these roles.

---

[16] My least favourite role was editing a journal. Literally, it is a thankless task (see Chapter 30).

12

Learning from a Trapped Moth[17]

Around thirty-five years ago, during a holiday, I experienced something that seemed simple at first but turned out to be meaningful. As I thought about it more, I realised it could offer a lesson for my work in counselling.

One evening after dinner, I sat in a small hotel alcove with a cup of coffee. As I relaxed, a large moth flew in and tried to escape through the main window, which was sealed shut. Seeing this, I opened a side window, hoping it would realise this was an escape route. Sadly, the moth, unaware of my effort, kept fluttering its wings, trying to fly through the closed window. Recognising I had to intervene more directly, I gently reached out to guide the moth towards the open window. The moth responded by lowering itself and fluttering more strongly. As I continued to guide it softly, it lowered further and fluttered faster. Eventually, I decided a more forceful move was needed, so I flicked my hand three quick times, successfully helping the moth escape.

Four lessons come from this situation. First, some people tend to approach problems in a stereotypical manner, relying on a single 'solution' they repeatedly use, regardless of its effectiveness. When this method fails, they often double down, putting even more effort into their unsuccessful approach. They are like a moth trying to fly through a closed window; when it fails, it flutters more vigorously.

---

[17] This is an updated version of a piece first published in Dryden (1993).

Second, some clients are very reluctant to give up coping strategies that do not work. When we offer gentle counselling and suggest better solutions, they often double down on their efforts to make their unsuccessful methods succeed, even if they acknowledge what we've said. The moth did react to my gentle approach by stepping back from my hand, but it responded by increasing its attempts to fly through the fixed window, trying to accelerate.

Third, although we may assist these clients in addressing their immediate problems through more intense interventions, what valuable lessons will they take away? When confronted with a fixed window again, how will the moth respond? Probably, it will act just as it did prior to our intervention—indicating that no new insights have been gained.

I concur with my former colleague, Richard Nelson-Jones, who believed that one goal of counselling is to empower clients with versatile life skills they can adapt in stressful situations. However, sometimes we meet clients resistant to this approach. In those instances, we must choose whether to tackle the client's immediate problem through a strong (and potentially dramatic) intervention or to continue with our usual methods without expecting change.

This brings me to my fourth and final point. Sometimes, in counselling, we need to take unconventional actions to help clients out of tough spots. I usually wouldn't go around flicking moths through open windows forcefully, but I was glad I did this time. I like to think that if I hadn't stepped in, the moth would still be there, fluttering its tired wings and hopelessly searching for an impossible escape.

We can only implement unconventional interventions if we're open to flexibility. Sticking strictly to our preferred guidelines may not always benefit all clients. Occasionally, we'll face challenges with clients' closed-mindedness, even when attempting to practice differently. Of course, deviating from our usual methods involves confronting discomfort that we usually prefer to sideline. This naturally brings us to the focus of the next chapter.

13

Embrace Discomfort as a Counsellor[18]

Many years ago, I served on a committee reviewing a counselling diploma programme. One objective was to help trainees develop a working style they felt at ease with. Initially, this seemed reasonable—after all, we don't want counsellors feeling uneasy in their practice, right? Wrong! I think that it is not such a bad idea if counsellors experience some discomfort. I support counsellors choosing their theoretical approaches, provided they recognise each has its limitations. To effectively serve a diverse client base, developing proficiency in various counselling methods is necessary. The difficulty is that some interventions might feel uncomfortable to employ. The key question is: will personal discomfort prevent us from growing professionally?

To determine the most effective interventions for particular clients at different therapy stages, counsellors need to study the work of practitioners from various orientations and explore counselling research. This involves extensive reading and reviewing research journals, which may require engaging with unfamiliar terminology, concepts and intricate research methods.

While different counselling and therapy methods often show similar effectiveness, evidence indicates that some specific problems require targeted approaches. For example, when working with a client who has a hand-washing compulsive behaviour, response prevention techniques are essential; without them, progress is unlikely, regardless of the warmth, empathy, or

---

[18] This is an updated version of a piece first published in Dryden (1993).

sincerity you show. Your supportive qualities may motivate the client to try response prevention, but they won't be enough to break persistent obsessive-compulsive habits. You might think, 'I'll refer the client to a specialist,' but consider the trade-offs. Choosing a referral keeps you in your comfort zone but also restricts your growth as a versatile practitioner, rather than embracing challenges that could enhance your skills.

The greatest excesses of counsellor comfort appear in staffing practices at certain agencies. Many years ago, I saw an advertisement for a Gestalt counsellor to join a team already made up of two Gestaltists. While this may seem reasonable, after all it is important for therapists to speak the same therapeutic language. But how does it benefit the client cohort, some of whom may not benefit from Gestalt work? It doesn't, in my view. And before anyone thinks that I have it in for Gestalt Therapy, I would feel the same if the therapists all practised REBT!

To genuinely respect our clients' uniqueness, we must recognise that different clients need different counselling approaches. This requires two main steps: first, individual counsellors should broaden their skills and methods; second, our counselling teams should include professionals from various backgrounds who are open to learning from each other and broadening the base of their practice. Although adopting these changes may cause discomfort, embracing this challenge ultimately benefits us as counsellors, promotes the growth of the counselling field, and most importantly, enhances the mental health and development of our clients.

14

When the Police Had to Evict One of My Clients[19]

Most of my practice over the years has been uneventful, and I decided that when writing this book, I would not make it about my client work. However, in this chapter, I decided to make an exception. The case I will discuss is so strange that it merits a chapter to itself.

I have always supported the principle that therapists should have professional indemnity insurance. While most counsellors conduct themselves professionally, it's impossible to predict exactly how clients might interpret our efforts. Here, I share a personal incident with a client that shocked me and temporarily led me to experience considerable worry. I was very relieved that I had insurance coverage.

To safeguard the client's privacy, I have altered some identifying details. I had only seen her once before the incident that I will describe in this chapter. She called me from a town in south-west England to schedule an appointment. I agreed to see her because she specifically wanted a counsellor familiar with the therapeutic approach I practise (REBT), which was not available locally.

Our first session was uneventful. She mentioned she couldn't attend regularly due to the distance between her home and my workplace but expressed a desire to meet occasionally on an ad

---

[19] This is an updated version of a piece first published in Dryden (1993).

hoc basis. I agreed, having used similar arrangements with other 'out of town' clients before, and they had always worked well.[20]

During the session, I helped her identify several self-defeating attitudes that hindered her progress and discussed ways to change them. She also casually noted that her previous counsellor, from a different tradition, was unhelpful. It's quite common for clients to seek me out when their previous therapy hasn't been productive for them, especially if they want to explore different orientations. We briefly discussed this, and everything seemed fine. After agreeing on some practical details, she left seemingly satisfied. I had no idea what was coming next.

About four months later, the client reached out again for another session, and I agreed to see her. She arrived carrying a large, heavy rucksack, which did not seem unusual at the time, as I assumed she had just arrived and planned to stay overnight with a friend in London, given it was late afternoon.

The second session was mostly uneventful. We discussed her efforts to apply what we had covered earlier, and I offered some suggestions for further progress. I also clarified a couple of minor misconceptions she had due to misunderstandings from one of my self-help books. She appeared quite satisfied and seemed to resonate with my approach.

Then, suddenly, she became quite agitated when talking again about her previous counselling relationship. She questioned how counsellors could practise an inferior method when a clearly more effective approach (mine) was available. She felt it was her duty to do something about it. She suddenly announced that she wouldn't leave my office until I had made a written promise to

---

[20] This was years before online therapy came into being.

retrain all practitioners of the 'inferior' method, regardless of whether they wanted retraining or not.

I tried to empathise with her distress and suggested discussing this issue at the start of our next session. However, she was immovable; unless I provided the written commitment she demanded, she refused to leave. Pointing to her rucksack, she even said she was prepared to sleep in my office until I agreed.

Recognising she was serious, I responded that since the session had ended and she was refusing to leave, she was trespassing. I warned her that I might have to call the police if she didn't leave immediately. Her reply was, 'Call the police, then.'

We sat silently for twenty minutes until the police arrived and escorted her out, telling her she could seek legal action if she wished. She stated that this was her plan and left voluntarily.

After regaining my composure—having been in shock for about an hour—I called my insurance agent to explain what had occurred. He said he would get back to me in the morning after consulting with the insurance company. When he did, he informed me that, although it was clear the client had no case against me, the insurance company strongly advised me to avoid further contact with her. Meanwhile, I was instructed to write a detailed report of the incident, just in case the client escalated her unusual demands.

To my knowledge, the client did not pursue any further steps, but two years later, she wrote me a very pleasant letter—although it didn't mention the incident—expressing her desire to resume therapy with me. I did not respond.

Counsellors already face stressful work, and incidents like this only add to that burden. Although most will never need to call the police to evict a client, there's always uncertainty about future appointments. You might never need to rely on professional indemnity insurance to handle a client's complaint, whether justified or strange, but if you're like me, you'll find it reassuring to have that coverage – just in case.

15

Controversial? You Never Know

As I will discuss in Chapter 30, I enjoy writing and have written a lot of books, chapters and articles. I particularly like writing up talks that I have been invited to give and finding a publishing outlet for them. In the mid-1990s, I was invited to give two talks. The first was a Keynote address at the European Association for Counselling in Dublin in November 1995. The other was the seventy-fourth in the Public Lecture Series of the Associates of the Student Counselling Service at the University of East Anglia in December 1997.

The Dublin lecture (as I shall refer to it) was, in my opinion, on a fairly uncontroversial subject. I called the talk 'The Counsellor as Educator'. My argument in that talk was that it is possible to think of the counsellor as a psychological educator and the client as a learner. I used REBT as an example. I said that once the client has agreed to proceed with REBT, the therapist can educate the client in their tasks as an REBT client. Later, I wrote an REBT workbook that outlined these tasks in a structured manner, explaining how the client can learn them (Dryden, 2001b, 2022a).

In the Norwich lecture (as I shall refer to it), I decided to take more of a risk. I titled my talk, 'Looking for the Good in Hitler and Acknowledging the Bad in Mother Teresa'. My argument in that talk was that the hallmark of good mental health is flexibility – a stance that can have such shocking implications. These include that no human being is bad and that even people like

Hitler have some good qualities (which I listed in the talk), and no human being is a saint and that even people like Mother Teresa have some bad qualities (which I also listed in the talk).

Over the years, I have learned not to take anything for granted in counselling and psychotherapy. My Dublin lecture was received very poorly by some of the audience, which was mainly comprised of person-centred and psychodynamic practitioners.[21] Indeed, one person loudly walked out during question time. In retrospect, the paper did challenge some traditional views of counselling, so maybe I should not have been surprised by the response. By contrast, my Norwich lecture was received enthusiastically and led to a lively and reflective discussion.

When the dust had settled after my Dublin talk I thought I had left controversy behind, but it was to raise its ugly head a decade later, as you will see in the next chapter.

---

[21] Undeterred, by the Dublin response to this talk, I decide to give it again as the 1996 Frank Lake Memorial Lecture at Bourneville College, Birmingham for the Clinical Theology Association where it was received more favourably.

16

The Professor and the Guru

In February 2007, an article appeared on page three of the *Times Higher Education Supplement* (THES) under the heading 'The Professor and the Guru'. I was the professor in that piece, and my friend Derek Gale was the 'guru'. The article stated that Goldsmiths was investigating me for my connections with Derek.

I had known Derek for several years. Through his publishing company, he had published several of my books, and he, I, and our respective wives had enjoyed pleasant dinners at each other's houses. I knew that Derek was a controversial figure in the field who often incorporated aspects of a therapeutic community into his work. I did not know that he had violated any ethical boundaries until I was contacted by the boyfriend of one of Derek's clients, who was concerned about Derek's treatment of his girlfriend and was supporting her and a few of Derek's other clients who were making a complaint against him to the Health Professions Council (HPC).[22]

When I refused to help the man who had contacted me, he complained to my college about my association with Derek and as far as I am aware, alerted the THES that he had done so. The gist of this man's complaint, when it came to light, was that my

---

[22] The Health Professions Council (HPC) is now known as the Health and Care Professions Council (HCPC). The case against Derek was later upheld, and he was removed from the HPC register.

wife and I attended a party at Derek Gale's house where some of Derek's clients served food and drinks to his guests.

I was visiting the Albert Ellis Institute in New York when I received a phone call from Goldsmiths, informing me that the Head of College (known as the Warden) wanted to see me and explaining the reason. Upon my return, I was interviewed by the Warden and reassured him that, although I attended the party, I was unaware that the waiters and food servers were Derek's clients. I believed they had been hired for the occasion from an external company. Additionally, I assured the Warden that if I had known, in advance, that these people were Derek's clients, I would not have attended the party. That was the truth.

The College accepted my explanation, and that was the end of the matter as far as they were concerned. As for me, this unsavoury incident can still be found on the internet, but at least if people want to read the THES article from February 2007, they will have to pay for it. In the spirit of fairness, I have included the link below for your reference.[23]

---

[23]   https://www.timeshighereducation.com/news/professors-links-to-guru-probed/207651.article

17

Narrowing and Widening the Lens in Psychotherapy

In my psychotherapy practice, I consider which lens best fits the client for each session. When I adopt a narrow lens, I aim to target what I call 'proximal' factors – elements directly involved in the specific issue the client wants to explore. These include what people present have said, the inferences the client drew from those statements, the client's actions in the situation, and their reactions to their own behaviour. In essence, proximal factors are present in the here-and-now of the client's experience.

When using a wide lens, I focus on understanding the distal factors related to the client's problem. These encompass childhood and school experiences that may influence the issue, potential genetic predispositions, personality traits, long-term relationship patterns and attachment styles.

A key aspect of this book and my approach to therapy is recognising that clients have vastly different goals. Some seek long-term therapy to reflect on their lives and explore comprehensive changes. Others come for help with a particular problem and prefer a brief intervention to resolve that issue quickly. Naturally, this means adopting a broader perspective in the first case and a more focused approach in the second. However, there are many cases when clients stay in therapy for a moderate period when both lenses are needed.

Let me be quite clear. I believe therapists should be able to adopt both types of lenses throughout their work. The choice of lens at any particular moment should be decided collaboratively with a client, rather than decided upon unilaterally by the therapist.

Using a wide lens in therapy can be problematic because it may overlook the immediate factors that are directly affecting the client in their specific situation. While focusing on distal factors might aid in gaining insight, it doesn't necessarily equip the client to address the proximal factors directly.

By contrast, using a narrow lens in therapy can lead to problems in the therapy because doing so may overlook important distal factors which keep leading the person into problematic situations.

Working with both lenses at different times, guided by the clients themselves, in my opinion, is the hallmark of effective therapy.

Encouraging Generalisation

In my training courses, I often share a story. Once, I saw a young man for therapy who was anxious about being criticised by his boss. We identified relevant factors, developed a solution, and he applied it successfully. About a month later, he returned, seeking help with criticism from his girlfriend. I asked if he used the same solution with her as he did with his boss. Confused, he asked, 'No, was I supposed to?'

This taught me a valuable lesson: people generally don't spontaneously transfer insights from therapy to other situations. They need active therapeutic help to do so. Therefore, when a client derives a lesson from a specific discussion (narrow lens focus), actively assist them in broadening their perspective to see how it applies to other relevant situations (wide lens focus).

18

Being Real in Therapy Sessions:
Using Self-Disclosure

After I graduated from the London School of Economics with a BSc in Social Psychology, I did a PhD at Bedford College on self-disclosure in psychology experiments. This led me, later when I became a counsellor, to think about the use of therapist self-disclosure in therapy sessions.

There is little consensus about this subject in the field. Those who favour the use of therapist self-disclosure argue the following.

1. When a therapist shares relevant personal experiences, it can assist the client in feeling more understood and connected to their therapist, thereby fostering a stronger therapeutic relationship.
2. Clients often feel more comfortable and willing to share when they see their therapist as relatable and human. Therapist self-disclosure supports this perception.
3. Therapists can demonstrate healthy coping skills and emotional regulation by sharing personal experiences, offering clients tangible examples. When doing so, it's most effective for the therapist to reveal their own struggles first and then describe how they used a strategy to resolve the issue.
4. Therapists opening up about their struggles can make clients feel less isolated and help normalise their own challenges.

5. Therapist self-disclosure may help balance the relationship with the client, potentially making them feel more at ease sharing their own problems.
6. Therapists can disclose their feelings about working with clients in therapy sessions, thus facilitating a here-and-now connection (Yalom & Yalom, 2024).

By contrast, therapists who counsel against the use of therapist self-disclosure argue the following:

1. Therapist self-disclosure might blur the boundary between professional and personal relationships, potentially undermining the therapy process.
2. Therapist self-disclosure may inadvertently redirect the session's focus from the client's concerns to the therapist's own experiences, potentially impeding the client's progress.
3. Clients may misinterpret the therapist's intentions or experiences, leading to confusion or negative perceptions.
4. Relying too much on therapist self-disclosure could limit the client's development of personal coping skills and independence.
5. If self-disclosure is seen as self-serving or poorly timed, it can reduce client trust.
6. Clients might feel overwhelmed by the therapist's disclosures, particularly if the therapist reveals unresolved problems or trauma.

Eliciting the Client's View and Agreement

One possible way to resolve this split is to consider both sides and recognise that therapist self-disclosure has advantages and disadvantages. Second, include the client in the decision-making process. Ask if they are interested in hearing your self-disclosure, and only proceed if they consent. Afterwards, check how they felt about what you shared. This approach puts the client in control of therapist self-disclosure, rather than the therapist.

Let me end this chapter with a personal experience of the negative effect of self-disclosure, one that has stayed with me for forty-four years. Between April and September 1981, I spent a six-month sabbatical from my post at the University of Aston in Birmingham at the 'Center for Cognitive Therapy' in Philadelphia. In fact, I was one of the first Britons to have an extended training in Cognitive Therapy under the auspices of Aaron T. Beck, the originator of this therapeutic approach.

During my time there, I saw many patients, but one who stood out to me was a middle-aged woman who had what Albert Ellis would have called 'abysmal low frustration tolerance'. Although clearly depressed, she would make herself unhealthily angry about a plethora of adversities. In one session, while trying to model good coping, I shared an experience where I struggled to deal with an adversity she was currently discussing, but how I eventually managed to overcome it.

In response, she said tetchily, 'Young man, I am not paying this clinic good money to hear about your problems. Please concentrate on mine.'

This taught me an important lesson. Always ask a client for permission to self-disclose and only do so when they have granted it.

19

Why I Don't Worry About What I Call What I Do

I have never been entirely happy using labels when describing what I do. This refers to both my professional title and my therapeutic orientation. With respect to the former am I a psychologist, a counselling psychologist, a psychotherapist, a therapist or a counsellor? I am happy to refer to myself or be referred to by any of these titles because it won't change what I do with clients.

I am aware, however, that titles offer people prestige and even financial benefit. I once wrote that the difference between a psychotherapist and a counsellor was that the former earns more than the latter even though they do very similar work in the consulting room (Dryden, 1998a).

When it comes to therapeutic orientation, my main allegiance is to Rational Emotive Behaviour Therapy (REBT) and yet I am aware that when I portray myself as such, I feel an internal pressure to deliver the goods, as it were, and practise a recognisable form of REBT. I have done many live therapy demonstrations and when I do them for an REBT organisation I am aware that my practice is different from when I do them in general. Here, the label constrains me.

One of my mentors, Arnold Lazarus who originated multi-modal therapy said that he was not comfortable calling himself a multi-modal therapist, even though he developed the approach, Rather, he was a clinical psychologist. I can understand his viewpoint. Describing myself by a title is more freeing than describing oneself as a particular kind of therapist and, as I discussed in Chapter 6, I have a strong tendency towards autonomy.

Interestingly, the label that I am happiest using when I am doing work that comes under this heading is single-session therapist. As I discuss in Chapter 21, single-session therapy (SST) is a mode of therapy delivery where the therapist contracts with the client to help them take away what they hope for from the session. The client is then encouraged to reflect on, digest and implement their learning from the session before deciding if they want to access more help.

In my view, SST is pluralistic and can be practised by therapist from different orientations (see Chapters 10 and 21). When I practise SST, I feel at my freest as a practitioner and only draw upon insights from REBT (my preferred orientation) if needed. And yet, I am not completely happy with the label 'single-session therapy'. No matter, how often I stress what it is (see above), people think it refers to a situation where clients are offered only one session and they cannot access anymore help even if they need to.

This is why I refer to my work in this area as 'ONEplus therapy'. The 'ONE' (in capitals) makes clear that my client and I are working to help the latter in one session while the 'plus' indicates that at a later date the client can access more help. While I prefer the term 'ONEplus therapy' to the term 'single-session therapy' I tend to use the latter as the former has not really taken off.

When I train people in single-session therapy (or ONEplus therapy). I am certain that someone will ask me, 'This sounds very much like coaching.' My response is that I am happy for the person to call it whatever they like as it won't change what I do.

20

Increasingly, I Have Become Uncomfortable Calling Myself a CBT Therapist

In the previous chapter, I discussed my antipathy to using labels when describing my work. Why then have I devoted a separate chapter to a similar theme – my increasing discomfort in calling myself a CBT therapist? I have done so for five main reasons, which I will discuss below.

Let me begin by saying that I do not regard Cognitive Behaviour Therapy as a therapeutic approach or orientation. I regard it as a therapeutic tradition, an umbrella, if you will, under which can be located a raft of different approaches, including Rational Emotive Behaviour Therapy – the approach with which I am most closely associated and arguably, from a chronological perspective, the first CBT approach (Ellis, 1957). Indeed, I edit a book series for Routledge called the 'CBT Distinctive Features' series, in which writers on the major CBT approaches outline the theoretical and practical distinctive features of each approach.

As I mentioned in Chapter 20, I was one of the first Britons to have an extended training in cognitive therapy, a major approach within the CBT tradition originated by Aaron T. Beck and developed by him and his colleagues at the University of Pennsylvania and beyond. Latterly, Beck's followers refer to cognitive therapy as 'cognitive behaviour therapy' and the former term has been dropped from use. This is confusing. Is

CBT a tradition or an approach and, if it is an approach, is it the one developed by Beck? If you practise CBT differently from the Beck approach are you a CBT therapist?

Now, while I am concerned about this appropriation of the name 'CBT' this is not why over the years I have become increasingly uncomfortable referring to myself as a CBT therapist. The following explains my disquiet.

Is REBT a Form of CBT?

About sixty years ago, there were only two approaches to CBT, Rational Emotive Behaviour Therapy (Ellis, 1962) and Cognitive Therapy (Beck, 1976). Returning to the present, if one were to consult what is perhaps the UK's bestselling text on CBT (Kennerley, Kirk & Westbrook, 2016), one would find no reference to REBT, no reference to Albert Ellis and if I am permitted to say so, no reference to myself. In the UK, at least, there is uncertainty about whether REBT is a form of CBT and many trainees on CBT courses have had little or no exposure to it. As an REBT therapist, I am uncomfortable claiming allegiance to a tradition that does not recognise me.

Therapeutic Style

REBT can be practised in a variety of different styles. We can use a Socratic style, a didactic style, and we can use metaphor and humour in either of these styles. Our choice will depend on what the client resonates with best and on what best promotes their learning. These days, CBT is almost synonymous with a therapeutic style originally known as collaborative empiricism.

If you do not adopt a collaborative approach with your clients, you are not doing CBT seems to be the message.

Now, remember what I said about my temperament in Chapter 6. I am largely autonomously driven. I do not take kindly to be told that there is only one therapeutic style that I can adopt with clients.

Manuals, Protocols and Therapist Drift

When I arrived at the Center for Cognitive Therapy in Philadelphia for a six-month sabbatical to learn and practise cognitive therapy, I was told to go away and read *Cognitive Therapy of Depression* (Beck, Rush, Shaw & Emery, 1979). Actually, this was a case of re-reading this book as I had devoured it when it was first published.

Subsequently, this text was referred to as a cognitive therapy manual for the treatment of depression, but it was not a manual. It was a well-written book that outlined treatment suggestions but allowed for therapist creativity. Current CBT manuals or protocols are very different. They are step-by-step guides which allow for little personal manoeuvre and woe betide the trainee who departs from the manual. They would be committing the sin of 'therapist drift', something that is to be avoided at all costs. Again, the autonomous part of me rails against such therapeutic straightjackets.

Case Formulation

The use of case formulation (also known as case conceptualisation) was not a prominent feature of the training that I received at the Center for Cognitive Therapy. This entered the CBT literature when Jacqueline Persons (1989) published her pioneering book on the subject. When you do a case formulation you construct an understanding of the client's problems and how they fit together. Predisposing and perpetuating factors are included and the results, with the client's active help are often presented diagrammatically.

Let me say that I have nothing against this practice. Indeed, I have presented an REBT approach to case formulation (Dryden, 1998b). What I do object to is the idea that the CBT therapist should not endeavour to help the client until they have arrived at a case formulation. For me this is rigid and handicaps clients who only want to attend and gain help from a few therapy sessions.

BABCP's Stance on CPD

I think that basically continuous professional development (CPD) is a good idea. It is important to keep up to date with developments in the field and I would add to gain an understanding of how other therapeutic approaches think about and address issues that I, as a CBT therapist come across in my practice. Thus, I see the value of adopting both a narrow and a wide lens when it comes to attending CPD activities (see Chapter 17).

I used to be a registered CBT therapist with the British Association for Behavioural and Cognitive Psychotherapy (BABCP). I resigned from this organisation when they would not accept as CPD training events that I attended that were not CBT. They were basically telling me how I should and should not develop myself as a CBT practitioner. You can imagine how the autonomous part of myself reacted to that!

21

Single-Session Therapy

In Chapter 21, I defined single-session therapy (SST) as 'a mode of therapy delivery where the therapist contracts with the client to help them take away what they hope for from the session. The client is then encouraged to reflect on, digest and implement their learning from the session before deciding if they want to access more help.' I also explained in that chapter why I don't particularly like the term 'single-session therapy' and use instead the term 'ONEplus therapy' to describe my work in this area.[24]

I became interested in single-session therapy, circa 2013, when I was beginning to think how I wanted to spend my professional time after I retired from my academic post at Goldsmiths University of London. At that time I was concerned about the amount of time that people had to wait for psychological help on the NHS in the UK and when they were seen, their first contact with the NHS service known at the time as IAPT (Improving Access to the Psychological Therapies)[25] was for an assessment of their problems to determine whether they should receive high-intensity treatment, low-intensity treatment or a specialist service.

After this assessment, another waiting period followed. By contrast, single-session therapy promised that therapy would begin at the first meeting and when SST was integrated into an

---

[24] However, I will use the term 'single-session therapy' in this book because most people know it by this name.

[25] This service has been rebranded, 'The NHS Talking Therapies for Anxiety and Depression'.

appointment-based service, waiting times for therapy fell dramatically and when SST took place in an 'open access, enter now'[26] service, clients could receive therapy during that visit.

This work appealed to me. I then realised that I was doing single-session therapy when conducting live demonstrations of therapy at training workshops that I ran over the years. While these demonstrations were 'one-off' sessions with no possibility of further sessions (at least with me), they did qualify as single-session therapy, at least to my way of thinking.

So I decided to devote much of my professional time after retiring from Goldsmiths, to doing single-session therapy, training people to do it, supervising some of those that I trained and writing books, chapters and articles on it.

Like several notable SST theorists and therapists (e.g. Moshe Talmon, 1990; Jeff Young, 2018; Flavio Cannistrà, 2022; and Michael Hoyt, 2024), I regard the single-session therapy mindset (also called single-session thinking) to be the foundation of single-session work (see also Porter, Pitt, Eubank, Butt & Thomas, 2024).

28 Elements of the Single-Session Therapy Mindset

The following are elements of the single-session therapy mindset that SST therapists keep in mind when doing the work: One session or more. Be open to both possibilities.

---

[26] The new name for a walk-in therapy service. The former name was deemed to be not invitational to those unable to walk.

1. One session or more. Be open to both possibilities.
2. It is possible to conduct a session without prior knowledge of the person.
3. Start therapy from the first moment.
4. View the session as a whole, complete in itself.
5. Potentially anyone can be helped in a single session.
6. Focus on the person, not the disorder.
7. The client-therapist relationship can be established rapidly.
8. Be transparent.
9. Single-session therapy is client-led.
10. The client decides how much therapy they want.
11. Identify and meet the client's preference for being helped.
12. Keep in mind the importance of negotiating an end-of-session goal with the client.
13. Keep in mind the importance of co-creating a therapeutic focus and maintaining it once it has been created.
14. Unless the client's preference is to the contrary, a single-session therapy session requires a structure.
15. Complex problems do not always require complex solutions.
16. Focus on what the client has done before concerning the problem.
17. Focus on the client's internal strengths and external resources.
18. Keep in mind that different methods can be used with different clients.
19. Be solution-focused, if relevant.
20. Promote in-session practice, if feasible.
21. Help the client plan for action.
22. Small may be beautiful.
23. Invite the client to summarise the session.

24. Encourage the client to specify takeaway(s).
25. Encourage generalisation, whenever possible.
26. Results are mainly achieved outside the session.
27. End the session well so that the client leaves the session with their morale restored.
28. Take nothing for granted.

FAQs about Single-Session Therapy

Most therapists usually hold a conventional therapy mindset when considering single-session therapy. As such, they frequently ask me the following questions at my training events. I include my answers below.

- *Question*: How can you develop a good enough therapeutic relationship in SST?
  Answer: By quickly identifying what the client's preferred outcome for the session is and working with them to achieve it. By being transparent about what you can do and what you can't do, while communicating empathy and respect.

- *Question*: How do you deal with risk in single-session therapy?
  Answer: In the same way as in other forms of therapy delivery. By working with the client to make them safe.

- *Question*: Can clients with 'x' disorder benefit from SST?
  Answer: It depends on what they want to achieve from the session. If their goals are realistic, then yes, but if not, then probably no.

For a complete list of frequently asked questions about SST and more extended answers, see Dryden (2022b).

22

Client-Led or Therapist-Led?

One of the main features of single-session therapy which, increasingly, I apply to all my therapeutic work is that it is client-led. If you ask therapists if their work is client-led or therapist-led, they would probably reply that it is client-led, but whether that is the case in practice is another matter.

There are several areas of therapeutic practice that we can examine to determine who is leading the way.

The First Session

Let me begin by considering the first therapy session. There are entire books devoted to what should happen in this session (Armstrong, 2000; Taibbi, 2016; Chow, 2018). Now one important question that needs to be answered theoretically and in practice is this, 'Should the therapist and the client get down to the matter of doing therapy straightaway?' By this, I mean that the therapist helps the client to articulate what they want to achieve from therapy, and the two of them immediately get down to the business of working towards the goal after contracting to do so and this happens in the first session.

If the answer to the above question is 'yes', then there is no time for activities such as case history taking, assessment of the person and of their suitability for therapy, and developing a case formulation. When a therapist and client begin therapy in moment one, engaging in these activities would be seen as barriers to doing this. If the answer is 'no', then one or more of the activities listed above can be carried out. The greater the number of these activities that the therapist and client engage with, the longer it will take the therapist and client to get started with therapy.

Albert Ellis used to recount that very early in his career he worked at a clinic that before therapy began, employed several lengthy assessment methods based on psychoanalytic theory (e.g., the Rorschach Test and the Thematic Apperception Test) and where an extensive developmental history of the client was also taken. This entire process would take several sessions and delayed the start of therapy. He noted that clients became increasingly frustrated with the process, which they did not understand and which, from their and Ellis's viewpoint, failed to benefit them. This taught Ellis the importance of beginning therapy as soon as possible in the first and perhaps, only therapy session that the person might attend.

While it may well be the case that a client wants to begin therapy immediately, it may also be the case that they may wish their therapist to take a case history, do an assessment and/or carry out a case formulation. How is the therapist to know which way the client wants to proceed? By following George Kelly's suggestion, 'Ask the client, they just might tell you.'

Goals

Goals are the reason d'être of psychotherapy. As I mentioned in Chapter 8, from a therapist's perspective, they are there to relieve the client's pain, to promote their growth or both, sequentially[27]

---

[27] Usually this sequence is 'relieve pain before promoting growth'.

(Mahrer, 1967). However, what is more important, in my view, is the goals the client wants to achieve from therapy.

While, from a working-alliance perspective, what is most important is that the therapist and client have shared goals for the outcome of their work together, from the present perspective, the question is this: who is leading this goal-setting, the client or the therapist? My preference is for the client to take the lead in doing so and if I have any concerns about the client's goal I will feel free to voice them and discuss the issue with the client.

Clients usually have more conservative goals than their therapists[28] and when a therapist leads the goal-setting process, the client's goal tends to be more ambitious than when the client is leading the process. Albert Ellis (1972) wrote a paper that is germane to this point. He wrote that clients often want to feel better (i.e., symptom change) while REBT therapists want them to get better (i.e., attitude change). I have no problem helping my clients achieve symptom change if that is what they want and if they don't want to opt for more ambitious goals, then I will respect that.

Helping Preferences

Norcross and Cooper (2021) argued that when clients receive therapy based on their helping preferences, they experience a better therapeutic outcome than when they don't. Thus, it is important for the therapist to establish what help the client is looking for from therapy at the outset or help them to discover this if they are unsure. This poses a challenge for therapists who practise a specific form of therapy. For example, what happens

---

[28] Apart from situations where the client's goal is unrealistic (e.g., 'Help me to never feel anxiety again').

when a client wants help that is inconsistent with the help usually provided by the therapy approach practised by the therapist? The choices here are:

1. The therapist offers the client help consistent with their preference.
2. The therapist refers the client to a practitioner who can offer therapy based on their helping preference if the therapist can't or won't do so.
3. The therapist persuades the client to change their helping preference to the one offered by the therapist's orientation.
4. The therapist proceeds to offer the client help that is consistent with their approach without discussing this with the client.

Client-led therapy would lead to options 1 and 2 being chosen. Therapist-led therapy would lead to option 3 being chosen. In my view, option 4 is not ethical since client informed consent has not been sought and, thus, this option should not be chosen.

23

On Being Strengths-Based in Therapy

'There is nothing wrong with you that what's right with you can't put right. [29]

I love the quote above. It shows a key change in psychotherapy, from focusing on what's wrong with people and trying to fix it with ideas from various therapeutic approaches, to recognising what's right with people and using this to help them deal with their issues. This latter approach has become known as strengths-based therapy.

Strengths-based therapy is grounded in a mindset, a way of viewing people that encourages them to see themselves as resourceful and resilient in the face of adversity or hardship. When they bring this mindset to therapy, they usually play a more active role in the therapeutic process than if they see themselves as vulnerable and lacking in personal resources.

I personally distinguish between tough-minded strengths and tender-minded strengths when working with clients. Under the heading of the former are strengths such as grit, determination, persistence, self-discipline, resilience, discomfort tolerance, distress tolerance and acceptance of life. Under the heading of the latter are strengths such as mindfulness, acceptance of oneself and others, self-compassion, empathy, mentalization, kindness,

---

[29] This quote has been attributed to Aldous Huxley. It is slightly modified from the original which is, 'There is nothing wrong with you that what's right with you cannot fix.'

care of oneself and others, and charity. I see these strengths as 'what's right with your client' that can be harnessed and used to deal with 'what's wrong with your client'.

There are several ways to encourage people to identify their strengths. You can (a) do so directly, (b) encourage them to think about how specific people would respond if asked to list your client's strengths, and (c) offer them strengths based on their narrative.

Asking Clients Directly

When you ask your client about their strengths, they may tell you, they may say they don't know or they may say they don't have any strengths. In the last two cases, here is how you could respond:

- When your client answers very quickly, you can say, 'You responded very quickly. Just take a moment and really think about the question before you answer it.'
- Ask, 'If you did know or you did have strengths, what would they be?'
- Ask, 'If you went for an interview for a job that you really wanted and they asked you what strengths you had, how would you respond?'
- Ask, 'Remember a time in your life when you knew what your strengths were, how would you have responded to my question then?'
- If your client's response is coloured by their current mood, establish this and then ask, 'If you were in a good mood and

I had asked you the same question, how would you answer it?'

Asking the Client about What Other People Think Their Strengths Are

Some clients may think that telling you what their strengths are is tantamount to bragging or being conceited, and this explains why they say, 'I don't know' or 'I don't have any.' They may also respond, 'That's not for me to say.' In which case, you can ask them what other people think their strengths are. Here are some examples:

- 'What strengths would somebody who knows you well and is objective about you say you have?'
- 'What strengths would your best friend say you have?'
- 'What strengths would the person who loves you most say you have?'

Once you have heard their responses, ask your client whether they agree with the person. If so, you can encourage your client to find ways of using these strengths in therapy.

Inferring Strengths from the Client's Narrative

Another way of encouraging your client to identify therapy strengths, is to listen for potential strengths in their narrative and raise this issue with them. For example, 'Listening to you tell me how hard life was for you back then, it occurred to me that you came through such difficult circumstances. What strengths do you have as a person that helped you to do that?'

If specific strengths seem apparent in your client's narrative, then you can put these to them. For example, 'I am struck by your empathy and kindness when you talk about your grandmother. Are these strengths in you that you can recognise?'

In addition to seeking out and utilising clients' strengths in therapy, it is also important to review their attempts to help themselves and capitalise on instances where they have helped themselves, which I will discuss in the next chapter.

24

Identifying and Capitalising on Clients' Previous Attempts to Deal with Problems

When a client seeks therapeutic help for problems or issues it is probable that they have tried to deal with these issues before coming to see you. Thus, they may have tried to help themself using methods that seemed intuitive to them, they may have sought advice concerning how to deal with their issues from friends and relatives or from professionals such as doctors and members of the clergy. They may have even have sought therapeutic help before.

How Has the Client Dealt with Their Nominated Problem Before?

Therapists frequently proceed with clients giving scant attention to the attempts that these clients may have previously made to address their nominated problems.[30] Such therapists argue that since the person still has the problem then, by definition their previous attempts at self-help or at getting help from others have been unsuccessful. While this latter point may be correct, it does not mean that the client has not done anything that may have been

---

[30] A nominated problem is the problem or issue that the client chooses to deal with at any given point of time. The client may well have other issues that they wish to deal with.

helpful. And if the therapist knows what the client has found beneficial then they can utilise this in the client's therapy.

It is also useful for the therapist to know what the person has done regarding the nominated problem that has not been helpful. This information is useful to the therapist so they can avoid using anything that is not likely to be helpful to the person.

Given this, it is beneficial to ask your client such questions as:

- What have you already done to address the issue that we have chosen to discuss?
- What has been helpful, even a little?
- What has not been helpful to you?

Has the Client Solved Similar Problems Before and Can This Information Be Used to Help Them with Their Nominated Problem?

Sometimes it happens that on investigation the client has solved a similar problem to their nominated problem. Let me provide an example.

Jane came to see me because she was anxious about starting her new job. On investigation she was anxious because she felt unconfident about being able to do the job. I asked Jane if she had ever had the experience of being unconfident about doing something, doing it anyway and ending up feeling confident, Jane said that she had, so I asked her to explain what she did that helped her to go from being unconfident to being confident about the task. After she had done so, I asked her what would happen if she applied the same process to her nominated problem. She said that it would be helpful for her. So, I helped her to do just that with a good outcome.

Has the Client Solved Dissimilar Problems Before and Can This Information Be Used to Help Them with Their Nominated Problem?

It is also useful sometimes to ask clients how they solved problems that have no clear relationship with their nominated problem. Thus, you can ask your client the following question, 'Have you had the experience of dealing successfully with an emotional problem that has no relationship with the problem you want to discuss with me?'

If they have, then you can tease out the factors that led to the change and then discuss with the client if they can transfer any of these factors as the address the nominated problem.

25

Helping Clients Get the Most from Every Therapy Session

Albert Ellis (1980) once wrote an important paper in which he argued that efficiency in psychotherapy was as important as effectiveness. In that paper, he outlined what he regarded as the criteria for therapeutic efficiency. These included 'such ingredients as depth-centeredness, pervasiveness, extensiveness, thoroughgoingness, maintenance of therapeutic progress, preventive psychotherapy, minimization of therapeutic harm, and encouragement of scientific flexibility' (Ellis, 1980: 414).

One ingredient that Ellis did not discuss in that paper was the efficient use of time, a subject that I have become increasingly interested in since becoming involved in the field of single-session therapy (see Chapter 21). In SST, as you do not know whether you are going to see the client again, you need to give a lot of thought to how the two of you are going to use the time that you do have together as efficiently as possible. This is why you cannot afford the luxury of taking a case history, assessing the client or getting an overall list of the client's problems and carrying out a case formulation based on this information.

However, my interest in time efficiency in psychotherapy goes beyond single-session therapy and I have written two books that consider this subject (Dryden, 2025b, 2025c). To give you a flavour of my thinking in this area, I have presented in Table 2 twenty-six principles that facilitate the efficient use of time in therapy for specific client problems (Dryden, 2025c).

Table 2: Principles that facilitate the efficient use of time in therapy

1	Find out what the person wants from therapy and offer problem-focused help when appropriate
2	Get informed consent
3	Adopt a client-led stance
4	Encourage your client to prepare for the first and subsequent therapy sessions
5	Use the working alliance concept as a general guide to your work with your client
6	Begin therapy with your client as soon as possible
7	Develop a problem list with your client and set an agenda for each session
8	Encourage your client to get the 'feel' of being in therapy with you, if necessary
9	Establish and maintain meta-therapy communication with your client
10	Identify and focus on your client's nominated problem
11	Be goal directed with your client
12	Problem assessment: be specific with your client
13	Be solution-focused with your client
14	Steps to take before helping your client find a solution
15	Help your client to select the solution that works best for them
16	Help your client try out the solution in the session
17	Help your client develop a plan to implement their chosen solution
18	Deal with your client's obstacles to change before and when they occur
19	Uncover and deal with your client's doubts, reservations and objections to therapy
20	Invite your client to summarise the session and specify takeaways
21	Invite your client to generalise their learning to other relevant aspects of their life
22	End each therapy session well with your client
23	Encourage your client to schedule sessions (or not) as they see fit
24	Encourage your client to engage in post-session reflection
25	Review periodically your client's views about therapy overall and their progress
26	End therapy well with your client

In this chapter, I will focus on two issues that I think are particularly germane to the topic of therapeutic efficiency: (a) encouraging clients to prepare for therapy sessions and (b) encouraging clients to reflect on, digest and implement their learning from therapy sessions.

Encouraging Clients to Prepare for Therapy Sessions

One of the major ways in which you can help your client to get the most out of therapy sessions is to encourage them to prepare for them. If you have made an appointment to see a client for the first time you can invite them to prepare for therapy by completing a pre-therapy form[31] such as the one in Table 3 (see pp. 93–4).

You can also help your client to prepare for subsequent sessions by completing a pre-session form[32] such as the one in Table 4 (see pp. 95–6).

I want to make about three points about the use of such forms:

1. It should be stressed that the main purpose of these forms is to help the client to prepare for therapist sessions so that they get the most from them.
2. Clients should be invited and not compelled to share their forms with their therapist.
3. It should be stressed that the completion of these forms is optional. The client should be told that it is fine to complete (and share) them and fine not to do so.

---

[31] In the actual form there are spaces for the client to write or type their responses. These have been omitted for space considerations.
[32] Again, in the actual form there are spaces for the client to write or type their responses. These have been omitted to save space.

Table 3: Pre-therapy form

We have agreed to meet for therapy sessions. Before we meet for the first time, I invite you to complete and return this pre-therapy form before your session with me. This will help you to prepare for the sessions that we will have so that you can get the most from them. If you want to share your thinking with me, please return it by email attachment before our first session so I can also prepare myself. It is fine not to do so. Also, please note that the completion of this form is optional.

Name: **Date:**

1. **What issue or issues do you want to focus on in therapy?**
    Be concise. In one or two sentences, get to the heart of each problem.

2. **Why is the issue or issues significant?**
    What's at stake? How does the issue or issues affect your life? What is the future impact if the issue or issues are not resolved?

3. **What do you want to achieve on this issue or issues by the end of therapy?**

4. **How have you tried to deal with each issue up to this point?**
    What steps, successful or unsuccessful, have you taken so far in addressing the issue?

5. **What strengths or inner resources could you draw upon while tackling the issue or issues?**
    If you struggle with answering this question, think what people who know you and who are on your side would say.

6. **Who are the people in your life who can support you as you tackle the issue or issues?**
    Name them and say what help each can provide.

7. **If you have nominated more than one issue in your response to Question 1, which issue do you want to tackle first in therapy?** Please explain your choice.

8. **If you have nominated more than one issue in your response to Question 1, which issue do you want to tackle first in therapy?** Please explain your choice.

9. **What help do you hope I can best provide you in the session on this issue? Please check the main <u>one</u>. Do not check more than one box.**

   ☐ Help me to develop greater understanding of the issue
   ☐ Help me by just listening while I talk about the issue
   ☐ Help me to feel heard and understood
   ☐ Help me to express my feelings about the issue
   ☐ Help me to solve an emotional or behavioural problem; help me get unstuck
   ☐ Help me to make a decision
   ☐ Help me to resolve a dilemma
   ☐ Help me by signposting me to the most appropriate service for my situation
   ☐ Other (please specify):

10. **What do you want to achieve by the end of our first (and perhaps only) session?**

11. **List below anything you think I need to know about you that if I did not know then, from your perspective, I would not be able to help you.**

Table 4: Pre-session form

Before you attend our next session, I invite you to complete and return this pre-session form. This will help you to review the progress you have made since our last session and to prepare for the coming session that we will have so that you can get the most from them. If you wish to do so, please return it by email attachment before our first session so I can also prepare myself. It is fine not to do so. Also note that the completion of this form is optional.

Name: **Session No:**   **Date:**

List below what you did since the last session to help yourself with the issue we discussed in that session.

1. **Since the last session, what progress have you made on the issue or issues you indicated that you wanted to focus on in therapy?**
    List each issue below separately and indicate the amount of progress you have made on it by using a 0% (no progress) – 100% (problem solved). Detail the factors that helped you to make the progress listed.

    - Issue 1:
    Factors that helped me make progress:

    - Issue 2:
    Factors that helped me make progress:

    - Issue 3:
    Factors that helped me make progress:

    - List other issues below, if relevant

3.   **What issue do you want to focus on in the upcoming session?**
     If this is different to the issue(s) previously listed, clarify how it
     relates to one or more of these issues.

4.   **What help do you hope I can best provide you in the session on
     this issue? Please check the main <u>one</u>. Do not check more than
     one box.**

     ☐ Help me to develop greater understanding of the issue
     ☐ Help me by just listening while I talk about the issue
     ☐ Help me to feel heard and understood
     ☐ Help me to express my feelings about the issue
     ☐ Help me to solve an emotional or behavioural problem; help me
        get unstuck
     ☐ Help me to make a decision
     ☐ Help me to resolve a dilemma
     ☐ Help me by signposting me to the most appropriate service for
        my situation
     ☐ Other (please specify):

5.   **What do you want to achieve on this issue by the end of the
     session?**

6.   **How have you tried to deal with this issue up to this point?**
     What steps, successful or unsuccessful, have you taken so far in
     addressing the issue?

7.   **What strengths or inner resources could you draw upon while
     tackling the issue?**
     If you struggle with answering this question, think what people who
     know you and who are on your side would say.

8.   **Who are the people in your life who can support you as you
     tackle the issue?**
     Name them and say what help each can provide.

Encouraging Clients to Reflect On, Digest and Implement Their Learning from Therapy Sessions

Similarly, I suggest that at the end of the session, you encourage your client to leave and reflect on the insights they have gained. They should consider how these insights might apply to other areas of their life and put this learning into practice, ideally in the presence of the adversity that is at the core of the issue. When they feel they have got as much as they can from these activities, they should arrange another appointment to see you. Once again, you should clearly communicate to the client that engaging in this process will help them maximise the benefits of the session, but that again it is optional, and if they want to book another session at the end of any particular session they are free to do so.[33]

---

[33] The exception to this is in single-session therapy, where the reflect-digest-implement-wait-decide process is an integral part of this mode of therapy delivery.

26

Learning by Watching, Listening to and Reading Transcripts on How Others Practise Therapy

While I have learned a great deal about therapy by reading books on the subject, I have learned most about how to practise therapy from watching and listening to others do therapy, from watching and listening to myself do therapy, and from reading transcripts of others and myself doing therapy. In this chapter, I will discuss what I have learned by watching, listening to and reading transcripts of others doing therapy.

'Gloria'

As I have mentioned, my initial counsellor training was on the one-year full-time Diploma in Counselling in Educational Settings at the University of London. This was based on client-centred therapy,[34] and although we studied other counselling approaches,[35] we were expected to practise as client-centred counsellors. As I mentioned in Chapter 7, while I resonated with client-centred *theory*, I did not resonate with the *practice* of client-centred therapy.

---

[34] I made the point earlier in this book that the terms 'person centred counselling' or 'person centred therapy' had not yet come into being in 1974. They began to be used in 1980 when Rogers (1980) published his book *A Way of Being*.
[35] The text that we used in the course was Patterson (1973).

One of the highlights of the Aston course for me was watching a film project called *Three Approaches to Psychotherapy* (Shostrom, 1965). These showed Carl Rogers (who developed and represented client-centred therapy), Fritz Perls (who developed and represented gestalt therapy) and Albert Ellis (who developed and represented what is now known as Rational Emotive Behaviour Therapy), work with a client known as 'Gloria'.[36]

It was the first time I had seen therapy *in action,* and watching Rogers work with Gloria reinforced my sense that I would struggle with the practice of client-centred therapy. I also did not resonate with the way Perls worked with Gloria. The person whose work I resonated with most was Albert Ellis, although the rest of the course members hated this session because it was so 'directive'. I think I allowed their views to colour my own, and for a time, I forgot about Rational-Emotive Therapy, as it was known then,[37] as a way of practising therapy.

Albert Ellis

I resumed my interest in Rational Emotive Behaviour Therapy in 1977 after attending a one-day workshop in Suffolk given by Dr Maxie C. Maultsby. I then spent the summer of 1978 at what is now the Albert Ellis Institute in New York, participating in several training courses on REBT and serving as Ellis's co-therapist in his therapy groups during the month of August.

During that month, I had a wonderful opportunity to watch and listen to Ellis practise REBT in a group setting. I learned

---

[36] These films are known colloquially as the 'Gloria films'.
[37] In 1993, Albert Ellis changed the name of the approach from Rational-Emotive Therapy to Rational Emotive Behaviour Therapy.

many things from Albert during that time in subsequent years, and whenever I visited the Institute, he would invite me to be an additional co-therapist in his groups and encouraged me to listen to audiotapes of therapy sessions that he used to put in a shoe box in the room that training Fellows of the Institute used.

I listened to many of these tapes and built up a picture of how Ellis practised and how superb his listening skills were. I also learned how focused he was in his work and, surprisingly, how much practical problem-solving he did with his clients in his group therapy sessions, which was not apparent from his writings.

Another thing that I learned from listening to these tapes became useful to me when I started practising single-session therapy (see Chapter 21). Ellis used to offer his clients the choice of booking a half-hour or a full-hour session. I noticed that in both, Ellis covered similar ground but that he was more focused and used time more efficiently in his half-hour sessions. This demonstrated what is known as 'Parkinson's Law' as applied to psychotherapy (Appelbaum, 1975). This principle states that the length of therapy expands according to the expectations set and the amount of time given to therapy.

From the mid-1960s, Ellis ran what became known as his Friday Night Workshops. Here, each Friday evening, Ellis would do two live demonstrations of REBT with volunteers from the audience on one of their 'problems of living'. I attended as many of these workshops as I could, as it was another opportunity to learn from watching and listening to him doing therapy. Ellis also used to do live demonstrations of REBT at his professional training workshops, which again I attended whenever possible.

In these demonstration therapy sessions, which were shorter than regular therapy sessions, Ellis's charisma and humour shone through. His work seemed to be inspired by the presence of an audience. I learned much about how to use humour in therapy by watching and listening to Ellis's demonstration work. In particular, I learned from him how to direct his humorous comments at a client's ideas and not at the person themself.

Much later, I followed in Ellis's footsteps by developing the habit of doing live demonstrations myself whenever I had the opportunity to do so (see Chapter 27).

In the early 2000s, I collaborated with Albert Ellis on a book of transcripts of some of his best demonstration therapy sessions (Dryden & Ellis, 2003). I often re-read these transcripts and never fail to learn something new when I do.[38]

Aaron Beck and David Burns

As mentioned earlier in this book, I took a six-month sabbatical at the 'Center for Cognitive Therapy' run by Aaron Beck in 1981. Although, I did not have much personal contact with Beck during this time, he did ask me to transcribe two videos that he had made with volunteer clients to show others how to do cognitive therapy.

This turned out to be a godsend. By transcribing the sessions, by hand, very slowly, I could see clearly what Beck's intentions were in the sessions and how he implemented them. I learned more about how to practise cognitive therapy from transcribing these two sessions than from any other of the training materials I was introduced to. In particular, I learned how to work Socratically, at a pace that enabled the client to think carefully about the questions put to them.

---

[38] Please see Epilogue, pp. 122–3, for additional comment on Ellis's later period.

During my time at the Center, I met David Burns, who had an office in the same building and had just published the best-selling book *Feeling Good: The New Mood Therapy*, a self-help book based on the principles of cognitive therapy (Burns, 1980). Burns invited me to observe and participate in several of his therapy sessions before I started work at the Center, with the explicit permission of his patients. I learned a great deal from him, particularly how to effectively handle a client's criticisms of the therapist's approach and how to use role reversal in examining a client's distorted thinking.

Here, Burns would articulate the client's thinking and encourage the client to play the role of the therapist, responding to this thinking. The resulting dialogue often led to more change than more traditional ways of dealing with negative thoughts. Finally, I learned how to use the downward technique[39] from watching Burns use it with his clients and from him encouraging me to do so with one or two of them. This experience informed my later work on inference chaining in REBT (Neenan & Dryden, 1999).

Arnold Lazarus

I then had the privilege of serving occasionally as co-therapist with Arnold Lazarus, who originated and developed multimodal therapy, an approach that Lazarus said was an example of technical eclecticism, where the therapist would draw techniques from across the therapeutic spectrum without being tied into the theory that originally spawned the technique. From Lazarus, I

---

[39] The downward technique is a method used in cognitive behavioural therapy (CBT) to identify core beliefs by exploring the meaning of negative thoughts. It involves repeatedly asking 'What does that mean?' about a negative thought until a core belief is revealed.

learned how to use a wide lens when considering the client's concerns (see Chapter 19) by utilising his BASIC ID assessment framework, which covers the seven major modalities of human experience[40] (Lazarus, 1989). I also saw how Lazarus's very personal approach to practising therapy facilitated the development of an effective working alliance (see Chapter 8).

In the next chapter, I will discuss what I have learned by watching, listening to and reading transcripts of me doing therapy.

---

[40] Where B = Behaviour; A = Affect; S = Sensation; I = Imagery; C = Cognition; I = Interpersonal Relationships; and D = Drugs or the physiological modality

27

Learning by Watching, Listening to and Reading Transcripts on How I Practise Therapy

During my training, apart from observing and listening to others conducting therapy, one of the most effective ways I learned to enhance my skills as a practitioner was to record audiotapes and seek supervision on them from a qualified supervisor who was at that time a more experienced therapist than I was. By listening to my tapes, my supervisor could suggest ways I could improve my skills, and often I could do the same for myself. I found that discussing my 'cases' without referencing what I actually did in therapy was helpful to better understand my client, but for enhancing my therapy skills, it was a poor substitute for listening to these audiotapes of my work.

After I finished my training, receiving supervision of my audiotapes continued to have a great impact on my development as a therapist. In this regard, I developed a co-supervisory relationship with Ruth Wessler, an REBT therapist and supervisor in Chicago where, for ten years, we supervised each other's therapy tapes by mail. This was an invaluable experience and one I heartily recommend.

Learning from My Demonstration Sessions

Since 2005, I have been doing live demonstrations of therapy with volunteers from an actual or online audience (see Dryden, 2021a). These demonstration sessions are one-off sessions with no prospect of further sessions with me. The volunteer knows this in advance.

Formerly, before I developed an interest in single-session therapy (SST), these demonstrations were largely on Rational Emotive Behaviour Therapy (REBT), but since 2014, as my interest in SST developed, they became more focused on SST.

Before the pandemic, my practice was to audio-record a session, have it transcribed and if the volunteer requested them, I would send them both the recording and transcript via a secure download. During the pandemic and subsequently when a lot of training courses are online, I was also able to capture a video of the session.

It is my habit to review each demonstration session after I have completed it. I either watch the video or listen to the audio and read the transcript simultaneously. In doing so, I focus on what I have done well and what could be improved, using the latter as a motivation to enhance my skills.

I have published several books of my transcripts, offering an ongoing commentary on my performance in the sessions (Dryden, 1996, 2018, 2019, 2021d, 2021e, 2022c, 2023, 2024b, 2025d). Here, is what I have learned by watching, listening to and reading transcripts of my demonstration sessions.

What I Am Good At

- I am good at ensuring that volunteers and myself share a common purpose for our session.
- I am good at creating a shared focus for the session.
- I am good at developing a good enough working alliance with volunteers to get the job done.
- I am generally pleased with the questions that I ask volunteers.
- I am able to develop a conversation with volunteers and don't talk too much in the session.
- I am generally good at helping volunteers to get to the heart of their issue.
- I am good at pacing the session and usually don't rush volunteers.
- I am good at using humour in sessions.
- Generally, I am pleased with my level of clarity in sessions.
- I am good at helping volunteers to access and learn from their previous attempts to help themselves with their nominated issues.
- I am good at helping volunteers to gain a more constructive perspective, which they can use to address their issue constructively.
- I am good at encouraging volunteers to specify their takeaways.

What Needs Improvement

- I need to be more consistent in explicitly agreeing a goal for the session with volunteers. Sometimes, I do this explicitly, sometimes I do so implicitly and sometimes I fail to do this at all.

- I need to be more consistent in encouraging volunteers to access their internal and external resources to help them with their nominated issues.
- I need to be more rigorous in encouraging volunteers to practise their selected solution in the session.
- I need to be more rigorous in helping volunteers to develop an action plan.
- I need to help volunteers generalise their learning more frequently.
- The area that I need to improve the most is not covering too much ground with volunteers in the session. When I cover too much ground with someone, I get in the way of them taking as much as they can from the session. Here, I fall prey to the 'more is more' principle of conventional therapy rather than practise the 'less is more' principle of single-session therapy.

In the books of my transcripts that I listed above, I generally receive feedback (two to three months after the session) that the volunteer was helped by discussing their issue with me. I find it comforting that although my skills can be improved upon in some areas, the work I do is good enough to help people benefit from a single demonstration session.

28

Creativity in Therapy

When used in therapy, the term 'creativity' often shows up in its adjectival form an is used in a particular way as in the following quote, 'Creative therapies enable you to express yourself in a variety of ways, often without using words, such as through painting, drawing, photography, dance, music or drama'[41] In this chapter, I will use the term differently. By creativity, I mean the generation of ideas, ways of looking at things or activities that are novel or that capture the interest of others.

As I emphasised in Chapter 22, I oppose the use of manuals or protocols in therapy. They aim to foster adherence to a specific approach, but, in my opinion, they hinder the imagination and negatively impact a therapist's creativity. However, I do not suggest that the therapist be undisciplined in their practice. In jazz, a musician must master the basics of their instrument before improvising. The same applies in therapy. A creative therapist has first refined their craft but then extends it by combining ideas that, at first glance, seem unrelated. Alternatively, the therapist shows creativity by presenting routine ideas in ways that actively engage the other person's imagination, whereas non-creative presentations would fail to do so.

I often strive to develop ways of working with a client that are unique to this person. When I am successful in this regard, I may create a technique to be used with a person that I may never use

---

[41] https://www.bacp.co.uk/about-therapy/types-of-therapy/creative-therapy/

again with anyone else. In doing so, I may draw upon any information that is available to me.

Let me provide an example. In one live demonstration with a volunteer that took place over Zoom, the person told me that she was struggling with distressing thoughts that she couldn't seem to banish from her mind or deal with adequately. Behind this woman was a poster with the following message, 'Feelings are much like waves, we can't stop them from coming, but we can choose which one to surf.'

I asked her about the message on this poster, and she replied that it was something that she uses to deal effectively with her distressing feelings. I then asked her to imagine that the poster said, 'Thoughts are much like waves, we can't stop them from coming, but we can choose which one to surf.' I then asked her what effect applying this message would have on her problem. She thought for a while and then said that she could imagine the effect would be positive. I then invited her to recall her distressing thoughts during the session and apply this message. She did this and found it was beneficial.

Humour

Ellis (1977) suggested that psychological issues often stem from a person taking themselves, others, or life too seriously. He believed therapists could assist clients by encouraging them to adopt a more humorous outlook, using humour themselves as a way of doing so.

My approach here is to first ask the client directly whether they believe humour has a place in therapy and whether they would appreciate me offering a humorous perspective on their problem if I do so sensitively. If I proceed, the effect of my humorous intervention is usually immediately clear.

Swaminath (2006) has argued that the use of therapist humour can be of potential help to the client in the following ways:

- It creates a more relaxed atmosphere and helps break down barriers.
- It can convey the message that the therapist is humane.
- It can build trust and empathy if used appropriately.
- It can help the client to relax and talk more freely.
- It can convey messages succinctly and effectively.
- It encourages communication on sensitive matters.
- It can be a source of insight into conflict.

In addition to asking your client whether they would welcome the introduction of therapist humour before you use it, it is also constructive to ask them for their reaction to your humour after the event.

Therapeutic Toolbox

Largely due to working online during the COVID-19 lockdown, I started to gather several objects that convey therapeutic messages. I placed these in a box, which I call my therapeutic toolbox. Here are some of these objects:

- *A magic wand* – to help clients set goals and to help them see that there is no magical way of bringing about desired changes.

- *A crystal ball* – to demonstrate that there is no way of foretelling the future.
- *A TV remote control* – that can change people at the press of a button!
- *A wooden letter I with dots of various colours* – to demonstrate the complexity of a human being, thus defying the application of a global rating that accounts for the person.

Whiteboard Animations and YouTube Videos[42]
My final example of creativity in therapy can be demonstrated by the following:

- A whiteboard animation describing single-session therapy
  https://www.youtube.com/watch?v=wIcuOVOABRw
- A whiteboard animation describing REBT's ABC framework of psychological disturbance and health
  https://www.youtube.com/results?search_query=windy+dry den+rebt+whiteboard+animation
- 'Moves like Dryden', a video outlining the ABCDEs of REBT in song.
  https://www.youtube.com/results?search_query=Moves+lik e+Dryden

---

[42] All three YouTube videos were accessed on 5 July 2025.

29

Repetition and Routine

Having written about creativity in the previous chapter, it may seem strange for me to write about repetition and routine, which seem to be the antithesis of creativity. However, as I am an advocate of pluralism (see Chapter 10), I hold a 'both/and' rather than an 'either/or' view of such matters. There is a place for creativity, *and* there is a place for repetition and routine in my life.

Repetition

In this section I will discuss the therapeutic value of repetition in two areas of my life that impacted later on my work as a therapist.

Implementing Michael Bentine's Attitude

In Chapters 1 and 2, I mentioned that in my youth I had a bad stammer and did not find NHS speech therapy very helpful to me. What was helpful to me were two things. The first was 'speaking on the breath', a method taught to me by Mrs Cosman, a private speech therapist, which I practised with repetition several times a day. The second was implementing an attitude that I heard the comedian discuss briefly during the course of a radio interview. This attitude, was, 'If I stammer, I stammer – too bad.'

I resolved to practise this, again with repetition, and as I did so, I dropped the safety-seeking behaviour that I used to avoid stammering, which served to maintain my anxiety. Intuitively I felt at that time that I needed to keep practising this attitude until my anxiety diminished and when this did happen my fluency increased and I stammered less.

Dealing with My Fear of Alsatian Dogs

When I was quite young, I was savaged by an Alsatian dog in the garden of a friend. After that event, I developed a fear of dogs, particularly Alsatians. Whenever I saw the latter, I would avoid them, which again served to maintain my fear. In my early twenties, I resolved to address this fear. Little did I know it then, but I had adopted an exposure programme. Instead of avoiding Alsatians, I sought them out even though I was anxious. I did this again with repetition until I noticed that I was no longer afraid of them any more (see Figure 1, p. 114).

As I discussed in Chapter 18, I am an advocate of what I call the coping model of therapist self-disclosure. Here, you ask your client if they are interested in your experience with the issue they have been discussing. If they are, tell them that you struggled with the issue and then how you dealt with it effectively, emphasising the therapeutic factors involved.

50 Not Out!

Figure 1: Windy with Alsatian

Therapeutic Factors

The therapeutic factors linking the two experiences that I have discussed above regarding repetition are as follows:

* Acknowledge fear (of speaking in public and Alsatian dogs).
* Approach the feared object (rather than avoid it) even though anxious.
* Acting in ways that are consistent with any healthy attitude being rehearsed (particularly in the case of dealing with my stammer).
* Take construction action *with repetition* until one is not afraid of the feared object any more.

In my view, and this is what I emphasise with my clients, the most important therapeutic factor here is repetition.

Routine

For me, a routine is a standard or a regular way of doing things. In one area of my life, writing, it does not involve a set time, while in another area, exercising, it more or less does.

My Writing Routine

As I will explain more fully in Chapter 30, I enjoy the process of writing. However, this process is underpinned by a routine. When I am writing something, which is most of the time, my routine involves writing a minimum of 500 words every day. I set it at this level because I will often exceed this minimum, leaving me feeling that I am ahead of the game, which for me is an important feeling.

My writing routine does not involve a set time that I devote to writing every day. It involves writing a set number of words every day, regardless of whether I feel like writing or not. This is a really important point – at least for me. The quality of my writing varies very little, and it remains the same whether I feel like writing or not.

My Exercise Routine

At the age of 75, which I am currently[43] I have a disintegrating disc in my back on my right side, a torn cartilage in my right knee, problems with both shoulders and a tendency to get calf injuries when I jog. To keep all these issues at bay, I perform exercises for each area five times a week. I do these exercises before going out six days a week, and I follow a fifty-minute routine that includes a brisk walk for five minutes, followed by five minutes of jogging. I do this routine before starting my working day. The times when I do my preventative exercises and my jog-walk will vary according to when I begin my jog-walk, but it will invariably be before my breakfast.

As with my writing, I engage with this routine whether I feel like doing so or not – as long as I am not ill. I do so because I do not want to experience the problems associated with the issues outlined above, and because keeping reasonably fit is important to me.

---

[43] I was born on 17 February 1950

Therapeutic Factors

The therapeutic factors linking the two areas I have discussed above regarding routine are as follows:

- Have good reasons for doing a routine and touch base with these reasons regularly.
- Be guided by what I call reason-based motivation rather than feeling-based motivation. Not 'feeling like' doing something is usually not a good reason not to do it if you have a good reason to do it!
- Incorporate a routine into your life. Do it at a time when you are most likely to do it.

And, of course, putting together the principles of repetition and routine increases the therapeutic potency of each.

30

Writing and Editing

Reflecting on my career in counselling and psychotherapy, I am perhaps most proud of my publication record. I have authored books, chapters, and articles both independently and collaboratively, edited books alone and with others, edited and co-edited professional journals, and edited several book series by myself.

I remember the joy I felt when my first article was published in 1977. It was entitled 'Client-centredness and Re-evaluation Co-counselling' and was published in a journal called *The Counsellor*, which is now defunct and could not be located in a Google search. I also recall the joy I felt when my first book, *Rational-Emotive Therapy: Fundamentals and Innovations*, was published in 1984 by Croom Helm. It was a collection of my previously published work and was the first book on what is now known as Rational Emotive Behaviour Therapy, written by a British author. It was republished in 2015 by Routledge in their *Psychology Revivals* series.

If you think that I am going to discuss all my publications, you will be delighted to learn that this is not my intention. I mention these two publications here because they were 'firsts' and, as such, have left an indelible mark on me.

What I will do here is to discuss briefly what I have enjoyed most and least about writing and editing. However, before I do so, let me make some general remarks about writing.

On Writing

There was little in my past to suggest that I would write as much as I have done. I wrote essays at school and university, and neither liked nor disliked the process. If I didn't have to write essays, then I wouldn't write anything. When I became a lecturer, there was an expectation that academics would do research and write. While I was an average researcher, I developed the habit of writing and found that I was engaged in a virtuous circle – the more I wrote, the more I enjoyed the process, and the more I enjoyed the process, the more I wrote.

I soon discovered that writing about a subject helped clarify my thoughts on the subject. I know that there are people who work out their thoughts on an issue and then write about it, but I have never been one of those people. Indeed, I enjoy the uncertainty concerning how an article, chapter or book will eventually turn out. For example, this book turned out quite differently from how I envisaged it when I first planned it.

I mentioned in the previous chapter that when I am in writing mode, which I am most of the time, I write a minimum of 500 words a day. So, there is a discipline to my writing, but one that facilitates my work. For me, 500 words is an easily achievable target and one that I often exceed.

What I Enjoy Writing Most About

When I stand back and consider my writings, those that I have enjoyed the most have involved me taking a Talmudic approach to text. Rooted in Jewish tradition, the Talmudic method is a style of textual analysis and interpretation that features meticulous examination of texts, logical reasoning, and open dialogue to uncover meaning and insights. This approach highlights precision, aiming to understand every detail of a text. I took this approach to two books that I greatly enjoyed writing.

The first of these books was entitled *The ABCs of REBT: Perspectives on Conceptualisation* (Dryden, 2013). In this book, I provided a close examination of the errors and confusions surrounding REBT's ABC framework, as expressed by authors of counselling and therapy textbooks, REBT therapists, including Albert Ellis, and clients. It involved me carefully categorising the errors and confusions and discerning patterns in the data. I really enjoyed the precision involved in compiling and writing this book.

The second book that I enjoyed researching and writing was one in which I critiqued Irvin Yalom's single-session consultation. Yalom, who is perhaps the most celebrated living psychotherapist,[44] is an advocate of long-term, open-ended psychotherapy who found in his eighties that he could not remember details of his long-term patients. Consequently, he decided to offer a yearly contract to new patients and close his long-term practice.

Then, as his memory continued to fail, he decided that the only way he could maintain his practice was to offer single-session consultations, albeit reluctantly, and wrote a book on twenty-two of them which he titled *Hour of the Heart: Connecting in the Here and Now* (Yalom & Yalom, 2024). My book, critiquing this work is called *A Critical Examination of Irvin D. Yalom's Single-Session Consultations: It is the Relationship that Heals* (Dryden, 2025a).

Concerned that people might use Yalom's book as a model for single-session therapy, which it is not, since his work was not based on the single-session therapy mindset (see Chapter 21), I wrote my book to highlight the advantages and disadvantages of

---

[44] As of 6 July 2025.

Yalom's work from an SST perspective. Again, I really enjoyed the close examination I made of Yalom's descriptions of his single-session work and finding themes in that work.

Another aspect of my writing that I particularly enjoy is the books I have written based on the transcripts of my REBT and SST demonstration sessions (Dryden, 1996, 2018, 2019, 2021d, 2021e, 2022c, 2023, 2024b, 2025d). What I enjoy most about this writing here is critiquing my own work and finding patterns in the feedback provided by the volunteers.

What I Enjoy Least about Publishing

Although I edited and co-edited several books in the field, it was not something I particularly enjoyed, and I no longer edit or co-edit any texts. I grew increasingly frustrated with chasing up contributors who failed to meet agreed deadlines. Additionally, several contributors failed to adhere to the agreed-upon chapter structure, despite giving their consent to do so.

When I write my own books, I am responsible for everything and don't have to chase myself, since I stick to my schedule and agree to follow my own structure. I can rely on myself!

However, my least favourite publishing task was editing a journal. Not only did I have to chase up contributors, I also had to chase up reviewers who were frequently late and sometimes very late with their reviews. Being a journal editor is literally a thankless task. When I stepped down as editor of the *Journal of Rational-Emotive & Cognitive-Behavior Therapy* after a ten-year stint, nobody thanked me!

Epilogue
When It's Time for Me to Retire

When I read Irvin Yalom's book *Hour of the Heart: Connecting in the Here and Now* (Yalom & Yalom, 2024), in preparation for my critique of this book (Dryden, 2025a) – see Chapter 30 – one thing struck me forcibly. Here was a man who loved doing long-term open-ended psychotherapy and could no longer do this work due to a failing memory. Then he could no longer offer patients therapy for a year, which he had been doing, due to a hastening of his memory issues.

To stay in the field and be helpful, he chose to offer patients a single-session consultation, a method with which he fundamentally disagreed. His stark choice: retire or stay in the field and do work that he would much rather not do. He chose the latter. At the end of the book, matters are taken out of his hands and after a final single-session consultation where his memory let him down altogether, he gave up seeing patients. However, as his co-author son, Ben, says at the end of the book, Yalom, who is now in his nineties, still plans to continue writing.

There was no evidence that any of Yalom's patients were harmed in his single-session consultations. Yalom decided to retire from practice when it became clear to him that he could not continue. In the case of Albert Ellis, this was less clear-cut. Ellis had always said that he was going to 'die in the saddle'. In other words, he had no intention of retiring. However, as Ellis aged, his hearing deteriorated, and partly because of this hearing loss, he became quite short-tempered in the demonstration sessions that he continued to do, some of which I witnessed directly.

As it happened, Ellis became ill so that he could not continue practising as a therapist. Still, he could write his autobiography in which he said unpleasant things about those who expressed concern about the wisdom of his continuing to practise, including me (Ellis, 2009).

Writing this book to mark my fifty years in the field has prompted me to reflect on questions such as, 'When should I retire?' and 'Can I rely on myself to be objective about this personal issue?' In a sense, I don't have the answer to these questions. However, the fact that I am asking them and not avoiding the issues involved is, I believe, a positive sign. Ignoring these questions won't help. So here is my current thinking, which, dear reader, may have changed by the time you read these words.

- I will stop working with clients when I stop enjoying this work. I will also stop if two people I know and trust independently tell me that it is time to do so.
- Since I consider working with clients to be the core of my profession, once I stop seeing clients, I will cease all activities that I believe are predicated on my ongoing practice as a therapist, such as training, supervision and writing about therapy. Once I stop seeing clients, I believe I can (a) continue writing in a general way as long as I do not write specifically about therapeutic work and (b) mentor younger therapists and help them develop their careers.

Many years ago, I worked at a private psychiatric hospital where the former director was allowed to continue seeing long-term patients. Every week, when he left the room he used, it had to be thoroughly cleaned and disinfected because he had urinated himself throughout the day. I remember thinking, 'God spare me from such a fate.' So, although I see retirement as an anathema, I really don't want to suffer the indignity of carrying on for too long.

I had planned to end the book on an upbeat note, so I will. The main title of this book is *50 Not Out!* Yes, I have reached a significant milestone. I enjoy all facets of my work – seeing clients, training, supervising, consulting and writing. I am physically fit and mentally agile. So, as I pointed out in Chapter 11, although there will be an end to my career, this is not it!!

We have now reached the end of this book. I hope you enjoyed it, and any feedback that you wish to offer me will be gratefully received at windy@windydryden.com

References

Appelbaum, S.A. (1975). Parkinson's Law in psychotherapy. *International Journal of Psychoanalytic Psychotherapy*, 4, 426–436.

Armstrong, P.S. (2000). *Opening Gambits: The First Session of Psychotherapy.* Jason Aronson.

Beck, A.T. (1976*). Cognitive Therapy and the Emotional Disorders.* International Universities Press.

Beck, A.T., Rush, A.J., Shaw, B.F, & Emery, G. (1979). *Cognitive Therapy of Depression.* Guilford.

Bordin, E.S. (1979). The generalizability of the psychoanalytic concept of the working alliance. *Psychotherapy: Theory, Research and Practice*, 16, 252–260.

Burns, D.D. (1980). *Feeling Good: The New Mood Therapy.* William Morrow and Company.

Cannistrà, F. (2022). The single session therapy mindset: Fourteen principles gained through an analysis of the literature. *International Journal of Brief Therapy and Family Science, 12*(1), 1–26.

Chow, D. (2018). *The First Kiss: Undoing the Intake Model and Igniting First Sessions in Psychotherapy.* Correlate Press.

Cooper, M. (2019). What is the pluralistic approach, and how is it different from integrative and eclectic practices? *Pluralistic Practice*, Blog, July 15.
https://pluralisticpractice.com/main-blog/pluralist-philosophy/what-is-the-pluralistic-approach-and-how-is-it-different-from-integrative-and-eclectic-practices/

Cooper, M. & Dryden, W. (eds). (2016). *The Handbook of Pluralistic Counselling and Psychotherapy.* Sage.

Cooper, M. & Law, D. (eds). (2018). *Working with Goals in Counselling and Psychotherapy.* Oxford University Press.

Cooper, M. & McLeod, J. (2011). *Pluralistic Counselling and Psychotherapy.* Sage.

Dryden, W. (1977). Client-centredness and re-evaluation co-counselling. *The Counsellor, 2*(1), 19–24.

Dryden, W. (1984). *Rational-Emotive Therapy: Fundamentals and Innovations.* Croom Helm.

Dryden, W. (1987). A case of theoretically consistent eclecticism: Humanizing a computer 'addict'. In J.C. Norcross (ed.), *Casebook of Eclectic Psychotherapy* (pp. 221–237). Brunner/Mazel.

Dryden, W. (1993). *Reflections on Counselling.* Whurr.

Dryden, W. (1996). *Rational Emotive Behaviour Therapy: Learning from Demonstration Sessions.* Whurr Publishers.

Dryden, W. (1998a). What I wished I'd learned during counsellor training. What I'm glad I did and didn't learn and what I'm sorry that I did. *Counselling Psychology Review, 13*(4), 15–22.

Dryden, W. (1998b). Understanding persons in the context of their problems: A rational emotive behaviour therapy perspective. In M. Bruch & F.W. Bond (eds), *Beyond Diagnosis: Case Formulation Approaches in CBT* (pp. 43–64). John Wiley & Sons.

Dryden, W. (2001a). How rational am I? Self-help using rational emotive behaviour therapy. In E. Spinelli & S. Marshall (eds), *Embodied Theories.* Continuum.

Dryden, W. (2001b). *Reason to Change: A Rational Emotive Behaviour Therapy (REBT) Workbook.* Brunner-Routledge.

Dryden, W. (2006). *Counselling in a Nutshell.* Sage.

Dryden, W. (2011). *Counselling in a Nutshell,* 2nd edition. Sage.

Dryden, W. (2013). *The ABCs of REBT: Perspectives on Conceptualization.* Springer.

Dryden, W. (2018). *Very Brief Therapeutic Conversations.* Routledge.

Dryden, W. (2019). *Rational Emotive Behaviour Therapy in India: Very Brief Therapy for Problems of Daily Living.* Routledge.

Dryden, W. (2021a). *Seven Principles of Doing Live Therapy Demonstrations.* Rationality Publications.

Dryden, W. (2021b). *Seven Principles of Rational Emotive Behaviour Therapy.* Rationality Publications.

Dryden, W. (2021c). *Seven Principles of Single-Session Therapy.* Rationality Publications.

Dryden, W. (2021d). *Windy Dryden Live!* Rationality Publications.

Dryden, W. (2021e). *Single-Session Therapy @ Onlinevents.* Onlinevents Publications.

Dryden, W. (2022a). *Reason to Change: A Rational Emotive Behaviour Therapy (REBT) Workbook.* Routledge.

Dryden, W. (2022b). *Single-Session Therapy: Responses to Frequently Asked Questions.* Routledge.

Dryden, W. (2022c). *'I Wish You a Healthy Christmas': Single-Session Therapy in Action.* Onlinevents Publications.

Dryden, W. (2023). *Single-Session Therapy and Regret.* Onlinevents Publications.

Dryden, W. (2024a). *Single-Session Therapy: 100 Key Points and Techniques.* 2nd edition. Routledge.

Dryden, W. (2024b). *Single-Session Therapy and Procrastination.* Onlinevents Publications.

Dryden, W. (2025a). *A Critical Examination of Irvin D. Yalom's Single-Session Consultations: It is the Relationship that Heals.* Routledge.

Dryden, W. (2025b). *Brief Therapy Informed by the Single-Session Therapy Mindset.* Onlinevents Publications.

Dryden, W. (2025c). *Efficient Therapy for Specific Client Problems: Making the Most of Every Client Session.* Routledge.

Dryden, W. (2025d). *Single-Session Therapy with Anxiety: An In-Depth Analysis of a Single Session.* Onlinevents Publications.

Dryden, W. & Ellis, A. (2003). *Albert Ellis Live!* Sage.

Ellis, A. (1957). Rational psychotherapy and individual psychology. *The Journal of Individual Psychology, 13*(1), 38–44.

Ellis, A. (1959). Requisite conditions for basic personality change. *Journal of Consulting Psychology, 23,* 538–540.

Ellis, A. (1977). Fun as psychotherapy. *Rational Living, 12*(1), 2–6.

Ellis, A. (1980). The value of efficiency in psychotherapy. *Psychotherapy: Theory, Research & Practice, 17*(4), 414–419.

Ellis, A. (2009). *All Out! An Autobiography.* Prometheus.

Flückiger, C., Del Re, A.C., Wampold, B.E., & Horvath, A.O. (2018). The alliance in adult psychotherapy: A meta-analytic synthesis. *Psychotherapy, 55*(4), 316–340.

Hoyt, M.F. (2024). *Single Session Therapy: A Clinical Introduction to Principles and Practices.* Routledge.

Jacobs, M. (2018). *50 Years of Counselling: My Presenting Past.* Open University Press.

Kennerley, H., Kirk, J., & Westbrook, D. (2016). *An Introduction to Cognitive Behaviour Therapy: Skills and Applications.* Sage.

Lazarus, A.A. (1989). *The Practice of Multimodal Therapy: Systematic, Comprehensive, and Effective Psychotherapy.* Johns Hopkins University Press.

Mahrer, A.R. (1967). *The Goals of Psychotherapy.* Appleton-Century.

Neenan, M., & Dryden, W. (1999). When laddering and the downward arrow can be used as adjuncts to inference chaining in REBT assessment. *Journal of Rational-Emotive and Cognitive-Behavior Therapy*, *17*(2), 95–104.

Norcross, J.C., & Cooper, M. (2021). *Personalizing Psychotherapy: Assessing and Accommodating Patient Preferences.* American Psychological Association.

Patterson, C.H. (1973). *Theories of Counseling and Psychotherapy.* 2nd edition. Harper & Row.

Persons, J.B. (1989). *Cognitive Therapy in Practice: A Case Formulation Approach.* W.W. Norton & Co.

Porter, S., Pitt, T., Eubank, M., Butt, J., & Thomas, O. (2024). An expert understanding of the single-session mindset. *Journal of Systemic Therapies*, *43*(3), https://doi.org/10.1521/jsyt.2024.43.3.02

Rescher, N. (1993). *Pluralism: Against the Demand for Consensus.* Oxford University Press.

Rogers, C.R. (1957). The necessary and sufficient conditions of therapeutic personality change. *Journal of Consulting Psychology*, *21*(2), 95–103.

Rogers, C.R. (1980). *A Way of Being.* Houghton Mifflin.

Shostrom, E.L. (Producer). (1965). *Three Approaches to Psychotherapy, Series I [Motion picture].* (Available from Psychological & Educational Films, 3334 East Coast Highway #252, Corona Del Mar, CA 92625).

Swaminath, G. (2006). Joke's a part: In defence of humour. *Indian Journal of Psychiatry*, *48*(3), 177–180.

Taibbi, R. (2016). *The Art of the First Session: Making Psychotherapy Count from the Start.* W.W. Norton & Co.

Talmon, M. (1990). *Single Session Therapy: Maximising the Effect of the First (and Often Only) Encounter.* Jossey-Bass.

Talmon, M. (2018). The eternal now: On becoming and being a single-session therapist. In M.F. Hoyt, M. Bobele, A. Slive, J. Young & M. Talmon (eds), *Single-Session Therapy by Walk-In or Appointment: Administrative, Clinical, and Supervisory Aspects of One-at-a-Time Services* (pp. 149–154). Routledge.

Yalom, I.D. & Yalom, B. (2024). *Hour of the Heart: Connecting in the Here and Now.* Piatkus.

Index

Page number in bold refers to illustrations

www.ingramcontent.com/pod-product-compliance
Lightning Source LLC
Chambersburg PA
CBHW050353280326
41933CB00010BA/1450